PROPHETIC PATTERNS

CHOOSING WHERE OUR BELIEVING LOYALTY BELONGS

MICHAEL FERGUSON

For the testimony of Jesus is the spirit of prophecy. – Revelation 19:10 (ESV)

For more information, email propheticpatterns5785@gmail.com.

ISBN: 979-8-89694-667-0 - eBook
ISBN: 979-8-89694-668-7 - Paperback
ISBN: 979-8-89694-669-4 - Hardcover

Dedication

This book is dedicated to Roger and Naomi Ferguson, my parents, who demonstrated God's hesed (חסד) love to me. Hesed encompasses more than just simple kindness; it signifies a deep, unwavering commitment to helping others, going beyond what is expected. Love and kindness is a way of life, not a strategy.

Gratitude

There are numerous people I would like to thank for being part of revealing what is expressed throughout the following pages. They all were guides, mentors, in various ways that have led me to a more robust search of truth. I began to consciously document my pursuit of truth in 2009.

A short list of those to whom I would express great gratitude include...

Clayt Irmeger – a mentor who ignited my pilot light for prayer into a source of purging and renewal. Well done, good and faithful servant!

Ed Garvin – a mentor who taught me that wisdom is a verb, not a noun. Wisdom is not an amount of knowledge. Wisdom is the accurate application of God's will.

Dr. Michael S. Heiser – a teacher and mentor who has, and continues, to expand my understanding of the unseen realm

Pat Williams – a mentor, an author, with a heart of a father, who invested himself into me for 2 ½ years

Chain Breaker Ministries and the men of Chain Breaker House who demonstrated the transformation possible through fully committed love

Jack Deere – an author who led me into my journey of actively listening for God's voice

Thomas Sowell – an author who expanded my understanding of reflection and discernment

E.M Bounds – an author of one of the most complete dissertations on prayer I've found

Andrew Murray – an author greatly gifted in expressing the essence of prayer

Julian Adams – prophetic group training to grow faith/relationship

John Eckhardt – an author who provided prophetic activation

Kurt Bubna – an author and mentor/coach in writing this book

Table of Contents

PART I
Setting the table

Have you ever perceived that you are being presented with a lesson in life you've been through before? Perhaps the location, or activities are different than before, and your view of it is from a different angle, perspective. But at some point, you realize there is an underlying pattern of information that communicates a message, a pivotal choice, that advises you which of two doors you should step through.

All of life is lived on levels and arrived at in stages.

There are two types of stories in the Bible – examples and warnings. We all have some of both in our lives. We can learn valuable lessons from both types of stories. The challenge for each of us to work to ensure that when the final chapter of our life is written, the balance of stories is on the side of examples.

Books are the windows of the world. They are a means to opening our minds to outside of what we are familiar with, inviting us to consider thoughts and experiences of others.

Literature forms character by allowing us to examine ideals and failures from a front row, intellectually speaking.[1]

Many people would recognize the name Vincent Van Gogh, and think of his paintings, which passionately portray vibrant colors and shapes that express what Van Gogh observed in life.

---

[1] Fant, G. (2013). *The Virtues of Reading Broadly.* https://www.uu.edu/journals/renewingminds/4/RM_Issue4_Dec2013_Fant.pdf

Although painted in 1889, Vincent Van Gogh's *Starry Night* appears to follow the laws of physics, specifically Kolmogorov's theory of turbulence, a scientific principle that was not formulated until 1942 (53 years later).

Most people are likely not aware that Vincent began his early adulthood as a priest who was passionate about ministering to the poor. He was so passionate about ministering to the poor, he didn't just visit them in his ministering, but lived with them. He took on, shared, their poverty in their daily lives.

Apparently, the church leadership objected to Vincent's chosen method of ministry and forced him out of the priesthood. Vincent redirected his passion to painting.

Vincent and his sister Wilemien were avid readers and often wrote each other to discuss the books they were reading. On Thursday, September 19, 1898, Vincent wrote to Wilemien. She was reading Tolstoy, and Vincent was reading Jules and Edmond de Goncourt (French authors).

So much the better that you prefer Tolstoy, you who read books above all to derive energies from them in order to act. I think you're right a thousand times over.

But I, who read books to seek in them the artist who made them, could I be wrong to like French novelists so much?[2]

Vincent read not to entertain ideas for activities in his daily life, but to find the author, the creator who was expressing who they are. Isn't that how the Bible should be read – in search of the author?

This book begins with believing that there is only one true God, who created all things and set patterns in place that govern their existence.

---

[2] *804 (805, W14): To Willemien van Gogh. Saint-Rémy-de-Provence, Thursday, 19 September 1889. - Vincent van Gogh Letters.* (2025). Vangoghletters.org. https://vangoghletters.org/vg/letters/let804/letter.html#translation

Mankind does not know whether knowledge is finite. It is likely that no two people possess the same knowledge, and it is impossible to prove that someone or something does not exist unless you possess all knowledge. It would follow that it is easier to prove someone or something exists than to prove the contrary. Searching, asking, are required. Therefore, ask yourself,

Is it possible that the knowledge of God exists in the portion of knowledge you do not yet possess?

There are things we believe because they are demonstrably true. There is hard evidence. These are what we call facts.

Then there are things we believe simply because they are asserted repeatedly, often with little to no evidence. These assertions are usually made with the intention of evoking emotion to enhance acceptance. These are called fallacies.[3]

Every experience you have had, along with the beliefs and values you associated with that experience, is stored in your subconscious. With each subsequent experience, the first thing you do with the input from the current experience is pass the data to your subconscious to compare with what's stored. Before you give the current experience any conscious thought, your subconscious hands your conscious mind an opinion about the current experience. Given that the opinion comes from your own mind, you find it credible. Unless you discipline yourself to give conscious thought to the current experience you remain stuck in a habitual rut. Surely, Paul could have been a certified psychologist when he wrote:

> [2] *Do not conform to the pattern of this world, but be transformed by the renewing of your mind. Then you will be able to test and approve what God's will is — his good, pleasing and perfect will. - Romans 12:2 (NIV)*

---

[3]   Sowell, T. (2011). *Economic Facts and Fallacies*. Basic Books, Cop

Michael Ferguson

This book aims to reveal some patterns embedded in the context of the original language and culture that the authors of the Bible were familiar with. The patterns are not hidden, but embedded. The pattern for finding them is ASK: Ask, Seek, Knock.

Who is God?

While we often default to assessing our experiences based on what we understand, or even just perceive, of the physical world, there is evidence throughout recorded history of an unseen realm – spiritual world. As Thomas Edison put it when asked whether he believed God existed:

You can't look at how the universe is organized and not believe that there is a captain on the bridge.

The Bible is God's inspired word expressed to and through mankind. He chose us to steward the Earth by sharing some of his attributes with us. What are God's attributes, and which of them does he share with us?

A.W. Tozer was a well-known American theologian. Theology is the systematic study of God, encompassing his nature, attributes, and his relationship with the world, particularly humanity. It's a discipline that explores religious beliefs and practices, offering various perspectives and interpretations. The term *theology* itself combines the Greek words *theos* (God) and *logos* (word or study). Tozer's two-volume set entitled *The Attributes of God* is a comprehensive dissertation that describes those attributes. The attributes God has not shared with use are:[4]

- Simplicity/Unity/Perfection
- Incorporeality

---

[4] Heiser, Michael S. 2023. *The Attributes of God*. <u>Awakening School of Theology</u>

- Incomprehensibility
- Uncreated
- Creator
- Eternality
- Immortality
- Immanence
- Transcendence
- Omnipresence
- Independence
- Infinitude
- Immutability
- Omnipotence
- Omniscience
- Providence/Sovereignty

Who are we?

As imagers of God, that reflect their creator/author, God has shared thirteen of the nineteen attributes described by A.W. Tozer.[5] The attributes Tozer identified as shared with humans are:

- Personhood
- Rationality
- Holiness
- Righteousness
- Justice
- Goodness
- Love
- Grace
- Mercy
- Freedom
- Truthfulness/Faithfulness
- Wisdom
- Order/Peace

[5]   Tozer, A. W., & Fessenden, D. E. (2007). *The Attributes of God. Volume 1, A journey into the Father's heart.* Wing Spread Publishers.
Tozer, A. W., & Fessenden, D. E. (2015). *The Attributes of God. Volume 2, Deeper into the Father's heart.* Moody Publishers.

These attributes define our identity. If these are what we have been equipped with to steward, we need to communicate them into the Earth realm.

We are not a body that has a spirit; we are a spirit that has a body.

What's the other option?

Disbelief in God, or belief that God is not real, is referred to as atheism.

Atheism is actually faith in certain miracles, although most atheists would likely object to referring to their belief as faith. Cliffe Kinnect identifies six miracles (a pattern) that atheists believe will lead to disproving God's existence.

1. Existence comes from non-existence
2. Order comes from chaos
3. Life comes from non-life
4. The personal comes from non-personal
5. Reason comes from non-reason
6. Morality comes from matter

Science requires measurement to assess and validate a theory. Given that atheists assert existence comes from nothing, they will never be able to produce evidence to support their theory.

Most people would accept claims that Homer wrote *The Iliad* and *The Odyssey*, yet the earliest claims of authorship emerged centuries after the works were written, with perhaps only five claims. In contrast, the New Testament by itself is confirmed by thousands of secular texts and archaeological discoveries dating within five years after Jesus' crucifixion.

What is prophecy?

As imagers of God, that reflect their creator/author, we do have an assignment, and the patterns of fulfillment of being appointed or anointed are revealed throughout the Bible.

Prophecy is often perceived as *predicting future events*. Formally, it is defined as *speaking divine utterances*. While prophecy can manifest as prediction of future events, that is not the core purpose of prophecy.

The Hebrew word *naba* is usually translated into the English *prophesy* or *prophesied*. It includes the context communicating *of proper behavior to a standard*.

> **5547** נָבָא *(nā·ḇā(’)): v;* ≡ *Str 5012; TWOT 1277— LN 33.459–33.462 (niph)* **prophesy**, *speak as a prophet, i.e., communicate a message from a deity, either of proper behavior to a standard, or of future events (1Sa 10:11); (1Sa 10:13)[6]*

Prophesying, being a prophet, is one of the offices the Apostle Paul identifies as gifts from God for the Church (Ephesians 4:11-14). In 1 Corinthians 14:1, Paul encourages the church at Corinth to prophesy - προφητεύω (*prophēteuō*). It is possible to prophesy without being a prophet.

---

[6] Swanson, James. 1997. In *Dictionary of Biblical Languages with Semantic Domains : Hebrew (Old Testament)*, electronic ed. Oak Harbor: Logos Research Systems, Inc.

4736 προφητεύω *(prophēteuō): vb; ≡ DBLHebr 5547; Str 4395; TDNT 6.781—LN 33.459* **speak inspired utterances**, *prophesy (Mt 7:22; Mk 14:65; Lk 1:67; Jn 11:51; Ac 2:17; 19:6; 21:9; 1Co 11:4; 13:9; 14:1ff; Jude 14; Rev 10:11; 11:3)*[7]

Why prophesy?

We are all leaders. The question for each of us becomes, *What direction am I leading?*

The best way to lead is by example.

The best way to learn to lead is to first learn what it is to follow.

The best leaders aren't focused on who is following them. The best leaders are focused on who they themselves are following.

We are promoted in life only by those whose instructions we follow.

The core struggle for every human being is between pride and humility. Pride is focused on self-interest. Humility recognizes the value in others as imagers of God.[8] Humility is also recognizing who God has made us to be as his imagers – our identity in him.

---

[7]   Swanson, James. 1997. In *Dictionary of Biblical Languages with Semantic Domains: Greek (New Testament)*, electronic ed. Oak Harbor: Logos Research Systems, Inc.

[8]   Murray, A. (2020). *Humility The Beauty Of Holiness*. Outlook Verlag.

What is a pattern?

A pattern is a model, image, form, plan, strategy, or map used to provide consistency in creating objects with intended purpose and value.

As imagers of God, we are capable of imagining. Not that we should pursue everything we can imagine. We must remember God and that role is as stewards of what he created. We need to know his ways so we can assess the things we imagine against what we know of him and his ways.

> **Pattern** *[Heb. taḇnîṯ, mar'eh; Gk. týpos, hypotýpōsis, hypódeigma]; also example (He. 8:5), fashion (Acts 7:44), form (2 Tim. 1:13); NEB also copy (He. 9:23), design (Ex. 25:9, 40), detailed plan (2 K. 16:10), outline (2 Tim 1:13).*

Exodus 25:9, 40 use Heb. *taḇnîṯ*, referring to shape or form, for the pattern that God gave Moses at Sinai for building the tabernacle in the wilderness (cf. the similar use of *taḇnîṯ* for a pattern of a pagan altar in 2 K. 16:10). Nu. 8:4 uses *mar'eh* (a sight, or the appearance of something) for this pattern, which Aaron followed in building the golden lampstand. The New Testament uses *týpos* ("type," "pattern," "model") in He. 8:5 (quoting Ex. 25:40, LXX Moses saw a representation of the true tabernacle in heaven (He. 8:2) after which the one on earth was to be modeled. It was made clear that although people would make the tabernacle, God determined its shape and form. Since God would be approached through the tabernacle and its services, the pattern had to be followed in every detail. Any deviation would result in the people's loss of the spiritual truths that a right approach to God would provide. He. 9:23 uses *hypodeígmata* for the "copies" ("patterns") of heavenly things in the wilderness tabernacle that as representations of heavenly realities foreshadowed the work of Jesus as the great high priest.

1 Timothy 1:16 sets forth Paul as "foremost of sinners" not only because he had persecuted God and His church but also because he was an "example" (*hypotýpōsis*; "pattern") of what God can do with any convert regardless of his past. If God had enough patience and love to forgive a blasphemer and persecutor such as Paul, He can do the same for all those who place no confidence in themselves but submit their will to His desires from day to day. Paul's experience is not the only example of God's perfect patience; rather, in every converted person God displays afresh the pattern that He follows when He reveals His love and patience to sinners.[9]

Translations

The Christian Bible has been translated into at least 3,756 languages, with 756 having full Bible translations, 1,726 having New Testament translations, and 1,274 having some portions of the Bible translated. Wycliffe Bible Translators states that as of September 2024, speakers of 3,765 languages had access to at least one book of the Bible.[10]

[9] Fagal, H. E. 1979–1988. "Pattern." In *The International Standard Bible Encyclopedia, Revised*, edited by Geoffrey W. Bromiley, 3:695–96. Wm. B. Eerdmans.
[10] https://www.wycliffe.net/resources/statistics/ . *Wycliffe. 1 September 2024.*

Growing up (which may be an assumption on my part), whenever I was in a doctor's office waiting room, I searched for *Connect the Dots* coloring books. Discovering a recognizable image by connecting all the numbered dots was a fulfilling adventure.

Connecting the dots has several purposes:

- **Understanding Relationships:** To *connect the dots* means to understand how different pieces of information fit together.
- **Finding Patterns:** It involves identifying recurring themes, connections, or relationships within a set of data.
- **Solving Problems:** It can also describe the process of solving a puzzle or mystery by piecing together clues.
- **Making Inferences:** *Connect the dots* can imply drawing conclusions or making inferences based on the relationships between facts.

I pray that what is shared in this book will help you to connect dots to reveal some images that are edifying in your life.

Note: Unless otherwise noted, quoted Scripture is taken from English Standard Version (ESV).

Fair question

M *ichael, how are you doing on what you're expressing in this book?*

The best response I could give is: Listen to me carefully, but don't watch me too closely. I'm working on this stuff too. We're all miracles in progress.

PART II
What does God want?

Words are important. Words are powerful. We don't necessarily each perceive the same meaning from the same word. We have different family backgrounds and experiences. Words are a major means of communication. Our behavior communicates. Nature communicates. The biggest problem with communication is assuming it has occurred. Effective communication requires effort from each participant.

While most translations of the Bible tell us we are created **in** God's image,

> *²⁷ So God created man in his own image, in the image of God he created him; male and female he created them. – Genesis 1:27 (ESV)*

it's important to realize that the word **in** can convey different meanings depending on context. For example, if someone told you they were going to *put the dishes in the sink*, the word **in** indicates location. If they told you *I work in the IT industry*, the word **in** indicates a role or assignment – that they work **as** a Project Manager, or **as** a programmer, or perhaps **as** a Network Engineer, etc. A better translation of the Biblical text might be that we are created **as** an image of God – a reflection.

God wants family. As his children, we carry his name and communicate the values our father teaches us. In other words, we convey family values. Communication can occur in various ways: verbal speech, behavior, art, written text, music, or our observations of nature.

We communicate by expressing data. Information is derived from that data. Derivation requires assessment, testing the data against what we've accepted as truth.

Dr. Michael Heiser taught that if we want to understand the Bible, we need to think like an ancient Israelite. Other than the books of Luke and Acts, every book of the Bible was written by an ancient Israelite, and their initial audience consisted of ancient Israelites. God did not place the authors of Scripture into trances while moving the quill held in their hand to write text, and then the person come out of the trance to wonder what they had written.

The Bible must be interpreted in context, and that context isn't your own or that of your theological tradition; it is the context that produced it (ancient Near East / Mediterranean).[11]

Though Biblical texts are considered canonical (divinely inspired), we know that ancient Israelites were familiar with and held to writings not considered canonical. Those texts inform us of what the authors of Biblical text were taught and how they lived – their worldview.

Both of my grandfathers died before I was born. However, I developed an understanding of their character by learning the ways of my grandmothers, my parents, and my aunts and uncles.

Since my early years were spent in the same town where my maternal grandmother lived, I was able to spend a good deal of time with her. She often told me that the two greatest influences in my life would be the people around me and the books I read

---

[11] Heiser, Dr. Michael S. June 16, 2011. *Heiser's Laws for Bible Study.* Naked Bible Podcast

(this was before twenty-four hour television with more than three available channels, the Internet, and cell phones).

My grandmother's house was three blocks from the railroad tracks that ran through town. At that time, *riding the rails* - climbing in box cars as a way of to travel across the country - was common for homeless men. I was having lunch with my grandmother when we heard a knock at her back porch door. Standing behind her as she answered the door, I heard the guest ask if he could do some work for her in exchange for food. After my grandmother told the man he could move a stack of firewood to the opposite side of her property, she led me back into the kitchen to prepare food for his wages.

I reminded my grandmother that the last time I was there and she answered a knock at the back door, she had asked a guest to move the stack of firewood from the opposite side of her property to where it currently was. I asked her why. That day, she taught me the importance of being rewarded for the value we provide to others.

It's a great feeling of accomplishment to finish a plan or strategy document for a project, identifying your goals, the people who need to be involved, and how you will address unexpected events. What is God's plan for the prophetic?

What's the plan?

God has never had a Plan B. His plan was, and still is, Eden, where he will live with his family.

A plan can be described to as a case or strategy that outlines who, what, when, where, and why of how something will be accomplished. It reveals a **pattern** of rules, criteria, resources, activities, and authority that can be replicated.

In this world, there are no solutions – only tradeoffs. In God's world, there are no tradeoffs – only solutions.

Plans require agreement among participants on how to address unexpected or undesirable events. They identify the levels of authority needed when such events occur. Plans require unity to achieve completion effectively.

All men are created equal, and endowed by their creator with certain unalienable rights.[12] Any community remains civil as long as the majority of its members adhere to agreed upon plans or patterns. Not only is God's plan superior than ours - since he is the author of life - he has full authority over the plan.

God delegated his authority to Adam and Eve as stewards of the Earth and informed them of the rules - a plan of intended, desired, results. Given our free-will, those results are not always what was intended or desired.

---

[12] Thomas Jefferson. 1776. *Declaration of Independence*

Pride enters

Just like a child, when you tell them what they are not allowed to do, they seem drawn to that very thing. Here is where the contingency section of the plan comes into play.

Why did the serpent engage Eve in conversation instead of Adam?

Scripture does not name the spirit of the serpent that deceived Eve. The name commonly applied in our day is Satan; however, that was not a formal name until the Latin translation of the Septuagint (the Greek translation of the entire Bible). What is used as a formal name, *Satan,* comes from the Hebrew *ha satan* (*the satan*), meaning *the accuser* or *primary adversary.* It refers to a member of the heavenly host whose role was to report to God what was happening on the Earth. Just like English, Hebrew does not tolerate the definite article *the* to procede a formal name. For example, I am not *the Michael.*

This is also true in Greek (New Testament) *ho* Σατανᾶς (*the Satanas*). Since English does not tolerate *the* before a formal name, English translations of Scripture drop the word *the.*

Eve was not named until after the Fall; before that she was referred to simply as *the woman.*

The serpent engaged in conversation with the one that did not have a name, the one who lacked an identity. If we do not know who we are - based on what we believe - we become more susceptible to everything the enemy tells us. The serpent aimed to steal the authority that Adam and Eve had been delegated, so he started where instilling doubt was more likely.

> **3** *¹Now the serpent was more crafty than any other beast of the field that the Lord God had made. He said to the woman, "Did God actually say, 'You shall not eat of any tree in the garden'?"² And the woman*

said to the serpent, "We may eat of the fruit of the trees in the garden, ³ but God said, 'You shall not eat of the fruit of the tree that is in the midst of the garden, neither shall you touch it, lest you die.' " ⁴ But the serpent said to the woman, "You will not surely die. ⁵ For God knows that when you eat of it your eyes will be opened, and you will be like God, knowing good and evil." ⁶ So when the woman saw that the tree was good for food, and that it was a delight to the eyes, and that the tree was to be desired to make one wise, she took of its fruit and ate, and she also gave some to her husband who was with her, and he ate. – Genesis 3:1-6 (ESV)

It wasn't until Genesis 3:20 that Eve was named….

²⁰ *The man called his wife's name Eve, because she was the mother of all living. (ESV)*

Interestingly, this passage now refers to Adam as *the man*. Was that indication that Adam had forgotten his identity by choosing not to speak order into the chaos before him?

The text also informs us that after eating of the fruit *she also gave some to her husband who was with her.* The English translation of *with* is the Hebrew *im* which means *in close proximity.* In today's vernacular, it could be understood as *shoulder to shoulder.* Adam's sin was in his silence – his failure to lead by speaking order into chaos. Paul tells us in 1 Timothy 2:14 that Eve was deceived, but Adam made a choice.

¹⁴ *and Adam was not deceived, but the woman was deceived. - 1 Timothy 2:14 (ESV)*

Can you imagine watching a basketball game where, after the teams go to their locker rooms at halftime, the goals are removed from the backboards? What will the teams think when they return to the court and see that the hoops are no longer on the backboards?

What's the promise?

God's promises to man are expressed through God's word. Some of these promises are communicated as covenants.

Covenant (בְּרִית, *berith* (Hebrew); διαθήκη, *diathēkē,* (Greek)). A sacred kinship bond between two parties, ratified by swearing an oath. Covenant making was a widespread custom throughout the ancient Near East and Greco-Roman culture, serving as a means to forge sociopolitical bonds between individuals or groups. God's covenants are prominent in every period of salvation history. Divine covenants reveal the saving plan of God for establishing communion with Israel and the nations.

An inadequate rendering of "covenant" as "testament" may obscure the theological meaning of the division of salvation history—and the biblical canon—into the old and new covenants. Covenant language is more prominent in the Old Testament, which reflects its futuristic character as "a story in search of an ending." The language of divine kinship (e.g., "father," "son") emerges in the New Testament, because Christ's fulfillment of the Old Covenant forges familial bonds of divine communion with all humanity.[13]

---

[13] Hahn, Scott. 2016. "Covenant." In *The Lexham Bible Dictionary*, edited by John D. Barry, David Bomar, Derek R. Brown, Rachel Klippenstein, Douglas Mangum, Carrie Sinclair Wolcott, Lazarus Wentz, Elliot Ritzema, and Wendy Widder. Bellingham, WA: Lexham Press.

The Abrahamic Covenant may be the best-known covenant in the Bible. There is a pattern connecting it to other covenantal passages.

> *⁷And he said to him, "I am the Lord who brought you out from Ur of the Chaldeans to give you this land to possess." ⁸But he said, "O Lord God, how am I to know that I shall possess it?" ⁹He said to him, "Bring me a heifer three years old, a female goat three years old, a ram three years old, a turtledove, and a young pigeon." ¹⁰And he brought him all these, cut them in half, and laid each half over against the other. But he did not cut the birds in half. ¹¹And when birds of prey came down on the carcasses, Abram drove them away.*
>
> *¹²As the sun was going down, a deep sleep fell on Abram. And behold, dreadful and great darkness fell upon him. ¹³Then the Lord said to Abram, "Know for certain that your offspring will be sojourners in a land that is not theirs and will be servants there, and they will be afflicted for four hundred years. ¹⁴But I will bring judgment on the nation that they serve, and afterward they shall come out with great possessions. ¹⁵As for you, you shall go to your fathers in peace; you shall be buried in a good old age. ¹⁶And they shall come back here in the fourth generation, for the iniquity of the Amorites is not yet complete."*
>
> *¹⁷When the sun had gone down and it was dark, behold, a smoking fire pot and a flaming torch passed between these pieces. ¹⁸On that day the Lord made a covenant with Abram, saying, "To your*

offspring I give this land, from the river of Egypt to the great river, the river Euphrates, [19] the land of the Kenites, the Kenizzites, the Kadmonites, [20] the Hittites, the Perizzites, the Rephaim, [21] the Amorites, the Canaanites, the Girgashites and the Jebusites." - *Genesis 15:7-21 (ESV)*

The action described was a common way to make a covenant in Near Eastern cultures. Halving sacrificial animals, creating a corridor with the halves, and the parties to the covenant walking the corridor as a way of stating *If I break this covenant, may I be rendered to pieces as these animals were.* There was water and blood present.

However, note that Abram was in a deep sleep before the corridor of sacrificial halves was walked. It was God who walked the corridor between the sacrificial halves. Since God cannot be rendered to pieces like sacrificial animals, the covenant cannot be broken. Yet God considered Abram and Sarai parties to the covenant. God's hesed love was gifting the covenant to Abram and Sarai in a way that would protect them.

> **2876** II. חֶסֶד *(ḥĕ·sĕḏ): n.masc.;* ≡ *Str 2617; TWOT 698a—***1.** *LN 25.33–25.58* **loyal love***, unfailing kindness, devotion, i.e., a love or affection that is steadfast based on a prior relationship (Ex 34:6, 7);* **2.** *LN 79.9–79.17* **glory***, i.e., lovely appearance (Isa 40:6);* **3.** *LN 88.66–88.74* **favor***, i.e., the giving benefits (Est 2:9), note: for another interp in Ps 52:3[EB 1]*[14]

When God made a covenant with Adam and Eve, he put Adam into a deep sleep to create Eve from a rib taken from Adam's side.

---

[14] Swanson, James. 1997. In *Dictionary of Biblical Languages with Semantic Domains : Hebrew (Old Testament)*, electronic ed. Oak Harbor: Logos Research Systems, Inc.

God entered the covenant by himself but considered Adam and Eve as parties to the covenant. God's hesed love was gifting the covenant to Adam and Eve. There was water and blood present.

When Jesus was crucified, his body was broken, and his side was pierced. There was water and blood present. He entered the covenant by himself and was in a deep sleep as the covenant was completed. Again, God was reaffirming and gifting the covenant to all mankind as he had promised Adam and Eve, then to Abraham and Sarah – to bless all nations.

Jesus was crucified alongside two thieves at a place called Golgotha (Place of the Skull). It was named that because viewed from a distance, the holes in the rock face appeared to resemble an image of a skull. From that distance, the cross on which Jesus hung on would have appeared to pierce the top of the skull. That fits the prophetic pattern God spoke over the serpent when he declared that Eve's offspring would crush the serpent's head.

> *[15] And I will put enmity between you and the woman, and between your offspring and hers; he will crush your head, and you will strike his heel." - Genesis 3:15 (NIV)*

> *[6] This is he who came by water and blood—Jesus Christ; not by the water only but by the water and the blood. And the Spirit is the one who testifies, because the Spirit is the truth. [7] For there are three that testify: [8] the Spirit and the water and the blood; and these three agree. - 1 John 5:6-8 (ESV)*

What we carry

Living in a physical world, it's understandable to seek scientific evidence. In fact, some scientists have attempted to disprove God's existence through scientific means. However, trying to prove that someone does not exist would require possessing all knowledge, making efforts to disprove God's existence unsuccessful.

James Watson and Francis Crick are renowned for their 1953 discovery of the DNA double helix structure. DNA, or deoxyribonucleic acid, is the molecule that carries genetic instructions for all known living organisms and many viruses. It's the blueprint (pattern) for life, containing the information needed for an organism's development, growth, and functioning. DNA is found in nearly every cell in the body and is passed from parent to offspring. This groundbreaking work revolutionized molecular biology and led to major advances in genetics, including techniques like genetic engineering and the mapping of the human genome. They were awarded the Nobel Prize in Physiology or Medicine in 1962 for their discovery.

Every cell of the human body (we have trillions of cells) contains our complete DNA genetic code. While DNA is very small, it holds a vast amount of information necessary for creating new cells.

The DNA molecule's double helix structure features *sulfur bridges* connecting the two strands, which follow a repeating pattern. These bridges are found 10, 5, 6, and 5 segments apart, a pattern that Dr. Yeshayahu Rubinstein has proposed correlates with the numeric value of the Hebrew letters Y-H-W-H (Yahweh). This pattern repeats throughout the DNA molecule.

10 + 5 + 6 + 5 = 26. The number 26 is considered a sacred number in Hebrew and is associated with the name of God, YHWH.

Twenty-six *esrim v'shesh (f) esrim v'shisha (m)* The numerical value of the divine and most holy name: YHWH (yod, hey, vav, hey) is twenty-six. The Torah was given on Mount Sinai in the 26th generation of mankind. There were 10 generations from Adam to Noah, 10 generations from Noah to Abraham, and another 6 generations from Abraham to Moses. Twenty-six means **oneness** (YHWH is One [Dt. 6:4]), but also carries ideas associated with the number four (The most holy name has four letters): dominion, authority, fullness, giving of Torah and Holy Spirit.

- 2×13=26, denoting that 26 is related to thirteen. Thirteen signifies *covenant, love, and unity.*
- Mankind is created in the image of YHWH (26). Not coincidentally, the Bible begins to describe the creation of mankind in the 26th verse of the Torah scroll in Hebrew. This is true even in English Bibles: *Then God said, "**Let Us make man in Our image**, according to Our likeness; and let them rule over the fish of the sea and over the birds of the sky and over the cattle and over all the earth, and over every creeping thing that creeps on the earth." –* Genesis 1:26

The DNA double helix consists of two strands held together by sulfur bridges (also known as sulfur bonds).[15] These bridges are not evenly spaced but follow a specific pattern.

Chemical processes are not random. They are predictable because they follow a pattern.

There is no known natural law through which matter can give rise to information.[16]

A code system is always the result of a mental process.[17]

---

[15] *The Chemistry of Oxygen and Sulfur*, Purdue University https://chemed.chem.purdue. edu/genchem/topicreview/bp/ch10/group6.php#:~:text=Because%20sulfur%20 does%20not%20form,form%20more%20than%20one%20crystal.

[16] Werner Gitt, *In the Beginning Was Information* (Green Forest, AR: Master Books, 2005), 80

[17] Werner Gitt, *In the Beginning Was Information* (Green Forest, AR: Master Books, 2005), 67-68

**

²⁰ For his invisible attributes, namely, his eternal power and divine nature, have been clearly perceived, ever since the creation of the world, in the things that have been made - Romans 1:20 (ESV)

When you plan a vacation, you first need to identify the destination. Once you know where you want to go, you need to determine where you're starting from. Then you must identify the mode(s) of transportation – walk , ride, or fly. The route you decide to take provides a pattern.

Adjusting the route

Whether you're walking along a hallway or you've boarded a commercial airline to fly from California to Hawaii, constant adjustments are needed to arrive safely at your destination.

Whether the pilot is flying the plane, or the onboard computers are controlling it, constant adjustments are needed for various of factors: the weight of the plane, wind, thrust of the engines. Otherwise, you're unlikely to land successfully at your intended airport.

Walking down a hallway, your brain assesses how close you are to walls or whether a door opens on the side of the hallway you're on. Again, we adjust our course based on what we see.

The same is true for all of life. Adjustments for various reasons are to be expected.

PART III
Biblical prophetic patterns

D r. Michael S. Heiser taught that if we could categorize all the prophets of the Old Testament as a group, it might be as *covenant enforcers*.

> *His voice speaks through chosen individuals to declare His plans, warn of judgment, and reveal the coming of the Messiah.*
>
> *It confirms God's sovereignty, calls us to righteousness, and assures us of His ultimate victory. - Dr Michael Heiser*

From Dr. Heiser's comment, this author has come to define prophecy as *reminding mankind of where our believing loyalty belongs*. We do that through patterns of our words and the way we live.

The prophets

The Prophets. The name for the prophetic books of the Old Testament. In the Christian Bible, this group is divided into the Major Prophets (Isaiah, Jeremiah, Lamentations, Ezekiel, Daniel) and the Minor Prophets (Hosea, Joel, Amos, Obadiah, Jonah, Micah, Nahum, Habakkuk, Zephaniah, Haggai, Zechariah, Malachi).

In the Hebrew Bible, the canonical division of the Prophets is called the Nebiim and includes all of these - except Lamentations and Daniel - as the "Latter Prophets." The "Former Prophets" in the Nebiim is made up of the books of Joshua, Judges, 1–2 Samuel, and 1–2 Kings.

Although the word "prophecy" often evokes images of people who predict the future, Hebrew prophets primarily anticipated the punishment of evil and/or a better life on earth for faithful Israelites (e.g., Isa 24:21–23; 26:1–6, 19; 27:12–13; 45:1–8; 60:1–22; Ezek 36–39; Zech 9; 14). They spoke the truth about the present and what would happen if people did not change their behavior and return to Yahweh's ways.

When Hebrew prophets did focus on the future, they usually were concerned with the short-term future. For example, they predicted the fall of Israel or Judah or the end of the Babylonian or Assyrian empires—events that ultimately fulfilled God's intentions or righteousness. At times, prophecies also concerned events far into the future. For instance, Old Testament prophecies do not reference Jesus by name, but they do speak about what a future Messiah or Suffering Servant would accomplish. The New Testament writers interpreted Old Testament texts as predictions of Jesus' birth, career, death, and resurrection (see Matt 1:22–23; Luke 1:32–33; Acts 2:22–35). Some events spoken of in biblical prophetic works have yet to occur, as with the New Testament promises of Jesus' return in Revelation (Rev 7; 22).

While the biblical prophets were primarily concerned with their original audience, their writings offer modern readers insight into God's will and divine justice.[18]

The act of speaking encompasses biological, psychological, and social aspects. The biological aspect involves the use of the mouth, lips, and tongue to produce speech. The psychological aspect centers on the intention to communicate, while the social aspects include the actual message conveyed, its form, the manner of delivery, the audience that is receiving the message, and the effect it has on that audience.

Most aspects of speaking have corresponding terms in both the Old Testament and New Testament. Both Hebrew and Greek have words for the parts of the body that produce speech: mouth (פֶּה *pe*; στόμα, *stoma*), lip (שָׂפָה *śāpâ*; χεῖλος, *cheilos*), and tongue (לָשׁוֹן, *lāšôn*; γλῶσσα, *glōssa*). These terms can refer to the literal, physical organs of speech, but they also can serve as a metonym for speech, language, or a specific characteristic of speech (e.g., *miśśĕpat-šeqer*, "deceitful tongue"; Psa 120:2). There are words in both languages that refer specifically to speech or speaking, including דָּבַר (*dābar*), אָמַר (*'āmar*), קָרָא (*qārā'*), παρρησιάζομαι (*parrēsiazomai*), and λέγω (*legō*).

---

[18] Redditt, Paul. 2016. "Prophets, the." In *The Lexham Bible Dictionary*, edited by John D. Barry, David Bomar, Derek R. Brown, Rachel Klippenstein, Douglas Mangum, Carrie Sinclair Wolcott, Lazarus Wentz, Elliot Ritzema, and Wendy Widder. Bellingham, WA: Lexham Press.

God is the first one to speak in the Bible; he "speaks" (אָמַר, 'āmar) and brings forth the entire created realm (Gen 1:3, 6, 9, 11, 14, 20, 24). People also possess the ability to speak and communicate with one another (Gen 4:8) and God (Gen 3:10, 12). The theological emphasis in the Bible is that a right way to use one's speech exists. That there is a right way to use one's voice implies that there is also a wrong way to use it.

Speech is used properly when it aligns with the nature of God and his commandments. This can be seen in the Decalogue, where some transgressions involve improper use of one's speech (Exod 20:7, 16). There are things that should and should not be said, and when speech is performed in concert with God's moral will, an act of worship occurs. If, as Paul says in 1 Cor 10:31, all human activity has the glory of God as its aim, then all speech that detracts from this aim would be improper—what the Bible calls sin. What makes speaking "improper" or "proper" depends on the intent and motivation of the human heart.

There are several significant forms of speaking in the Bible, especially words related to worship and prophecy or preaching. The prophets are involved in both the reception and proclamation of the "word of the Lord" (*děbar yhwh*); some oracles were to encourage (Amos 9:11–15) and some to condemn (Hos 5). Similarly, in the New Testament, the apostles and elders preached the word of God (i.e., the gospel of Jesus Christ; Mark 16:15; Rom 1:15, 20; 2 Tim 4:2). Paul argued that faith cannot exist apart from "hearing" the gospel, providing ample reason for him to verbally share the gospel with everyone he interacted with (Rom 10).

Old Testament

God spoke (*amar*) to create. אָמַר ('āmar). vb. **to say.** *A common verb for speaking, used for everyday speech, to give orders, or to indicate thoughtful reflection.*

This verb generally refers to verbal communication. When 'āmar is used, the content of what is being said is assumed to be both heard and understood. The contextual usage of 'āmar typically involves a subject that speaks, the information that is spoken, and an object that hears and understands that information.

The word is common, and its usage is fairly generic. However, 'āmar can be used with subtle nuances in varying contexts. For example, 'āmar in Gen 22:2 refers to how God will "show" (אֹמַר, 'ōmar) Abraham the specific mountain on which he must sacrifice his son (see also Num 21:14). Moreover, one finds 'āmar used in relation to the special act of giving someone a (new) name (e.g., Gen 32:29; Isa 4:3; 32:5; 61:6). The term also is employed to express concepts of imputation, such as oaths, promises, blessings, and curses (Gen 21:22–33; 26:15–33; 27; 33:1–18; 1 Kgs 1:28–30; 3:16–28; 2 Kgs 2:8–10; 2 Sam 15:10; 16:5–13; Psa 41:6; Jer 26:7–19).

> אֹמֶר *('ōmer). n. masc.* **speech, command, promise, matter.** *Refers generally to a type of speech about God, ranging from God's glory and power to his promises, or a matter or subject on which a decision must be made.*

The noun 'ōmer appears six times in Old Testament poetic texts (Pss 19:3–4; 68:11; 77:9; Job 22:28; Hab 3:9), and nearly every example has a different nuance. In Psalm 19:3–4, a hymn of creation celebrating God's glory, 'ōmer means "speech." Psalm 77:9, where the context is a prayer and 'ōmer is in parallelism with חֶסֶד (*hesed*, "loving-kindness"), 'ōmer means "promise." In

Job 22:28 'ōmer indicates the "matter" or "business" that must be put into action. The meaning of 'ōmer in Hab 3:9 is unclear.[19]

Note that the Hebrew practice to counting the omer during the fifty days between Passover and Shavuot (Pentecost) includes speaking blessings of God each of those fifty days.

New Testament

While there are numerous Greek words used in New Testament text to convey the concept of speech, the most well-known might be *logos*.

λόγος (*logos*). n. masc. **word, statement, speech.** *Refers to a word that is spoken, a type of word or speech, or an expression of some sort.*

Logos has a wide range of meaning, so only close attention to context can uncover the word's precise nuance. As it relates to speaking, *logos* often refers to actual spoken "words" (i.e., the linguistic production of speech; Matt 8:8; Rom 15:18; Col 3:17; 2 Thess 2:17; 1 John 3:18). The noun also is used with other modifiers to describe one's words in a collective sense (often translated "speech"), bringing out the nature, conduct, or manner of one's words (1 Cor 1:5, 17; 2:1; 14:9; 2 Cor 10:10; 11:6; Col 4:6; 1 Thess 2:5; 1 Tim 4:12; Titus 2:8). Also relevant is the way *logos* refers to a "statement" or "assertion" of definite content (Matt 12:32; 15:12; Acts 11:2). When used in the plural (λόγοι, *logoi*), the noun refers either to words spoken on various occasions or to speeches made at different times (Matt 12:37; Mark 13:31; Luke 21:33; Acts 2:40; 7:22). *Logos* often is used to refer to the revelation of God, especially in the phrase "word of God" (e.g., Matt 15:6; Mark 7:13). This theological use of *logos* appears

---

[19] Atwood, Preston Lee. 2014. "Speaking." In *Lexham Theological Wordbook*, edited by Douglas Mangum, Derek R. Brown, Rachel Klippenstein, and Rebekah Hurst. Lexham Bible Reference Series. Bellingham, WA: Lexham Press.

frequently, sometimes referring more generally to God's word, command, or commission (John 8:55) or to the divine revelation through Christ and his messengers (Titus 1:3).[20]

Some early Church Fathers, beginning in the second century, sought to move the Church away from the Hebrew language and Judaism, as speaking and understanding the language and cultural practices were not part of their congregational experiences. Three early events exemplify this shift:

- By the 4th century there was a strong move to an anti-Jewishness stance in the Church.
- AD 306 – The Council of Elvira forbade Christians from receiving a blessing from Jews.
- AD 325 – Constantine called the Council of Nicaea together and urged them to disassociate from anything Jewish. No Jewish bishops were invited to the council. The Western calendar for observing the resurrection of Jesus was one of the outcomes of the council.

Authority and Power

Authority is more significant than power.

It's easy for us to focus on power because we accomplish work by applying it. However, power applied without authority is illegitimate and unrighteous. Authority, whether in our physical world or the spiritual realm, is determined by proximity to the author. Every degree of authority, defined by one's position in relation to the author, comes with a corresponding degree of power. A closer relationship to the author grants access to a greater degree of power.

---

[20] Atwood, Preston Lee. 2014. "Speaking." In *Lexham Theological Wordbook*, edited by Douglas Mangum, Derek R. Brown, Rachel Klippenstein, and Rebekah Hurst. Lexham Bible Reference Series. Bellingham, WA: Lexham Press.

When the devil tempted Jesus, he offered Jesus all the kingdoms of the earth if Jesus would worship him. This offer was legally valid because, at that time the devil held authority over all the kingdoms. Jesus likely understood that, like Adam, if he accepted the offer, he would relinquish his authority in heaven, which is the very desire Scripture attributes to the devil.

Before Jesus ascended, he told his disciples that all authority in Heaven and Earth had been granted to him. He didn't need to mention power, as it was understood that with all authority came all power.

The Hebrew word for *authority* is *reshut* (רשות), which translates to *permission, authority,* or *domain,* comes from the root *rasha* (רשה), meaning *to authorize, permit,* or *allow.*

The Greek word for *authority* is ἐξουσία (*exousia*), referring to *right, judge, jurisdiction,* or *to rule.* The word *power* is usually used to describe that right.

The Hebrew word for *power* is כוח (*koach*) which can also mean *strength* or *force.* A related word, תֹּקֶף (*toqeph*), translates to *power, strength,* or *energy.* The word *El* (אֵל) in Hebrew, while primarily meaning *God,* also has a root meaning of *might, strength, power,* referring to an effect.

The Greek word for *power* is δύναμις (dynamis), which translates to *ability, might,* or *deed.* Like its Hebrew counterpart, this word is refers to an effect and is the root for the English word *dynamite.*

The New Testament references the words authority and power more frequently than the Old Testament. The original Greek text often interchanges *exousia* and *dynamis*, indicating they are closely related concepts. At times, translations of the original texts render *power* from *exousia*, and *authority* from *dynamis*.

Intercession

Prayer is an integral component of the prophetic. Prayer is the lungs through which the Holy Spirit breathes. Intercessory prayer is the highest form of prayer.

Rees Howells, a well-known intercessor, taught that true intercession is modeled after Jesus' work of intercession. It's an assignment that we either accept or decline. If we accept it, we do so with the understanding that it is ours until victory is realized. This involves submitting ourselves fully to the Holy Spirit's guidance. It has three stages:

1. Identification
2. Agony
3. Authority

We first need to identify with the person(s) or situation to understand the issue. Once we've gained that understanding, we begin to assist in bearing the burden. It is only after bearing the burden to some degree that we obtain a position of authority over it. The authority isn't truly ours; it comes from submitting to God's Holy Spirit to work/speak through us.

The Hebrew word *paga* is translated into various forms of the English *intercede*. *Paga!* is used today as an Israeli military command to *load your weapon*. It's also used to mean *hit the target* and *create a meeting*. When we *paga* (intercede), we are creating a meeting between the Holy Spirit and those we intercede for.

Who may prophesy?

If prophecy consists of divine utterances, then both God and mankind can prophesy. Utterances can be expressed in numerous ways: verbal speech, written words, dancing, singing, painting, sculpture, even simply our physical posture or behavior. Even nature, God's creation, speaks.

> [1] *The heavens declare the glory of God,*
> *and the sky above proclaims his handiwork.*
> [2] *Day to day pours out speech,*
> *and night to night reveals knowledge.*
> [3] *There is no speech, nor are there words,*
> *whose voice is not heard.*
> [4] *Their voice goes out through all the earth,*
> *and their words to the end of the world.*
> *- Psalm 19:1-4 (ESV)*

This doesn't leave anyone in the family of God out. **All may prophesy!**

> [31] *For you can all prophesy one by one, so that all may learn and all be encouraged,* [32] *and the spirits of prophets are subject to prophets.* [33] *For God is not a God of confusion but of peace. - 1 Corinthians 14:31-33 (ESV)*

Types of prophets

There are different ways the prophetic gifting flows, and individuals may flow in multiple ways of prophecy.

- **Nabi** (bubble up) נָבִיא (*nā·ḇî(')*): This stream is characterized by an unction from within that allows for vocalized prophecy, likened to a flow of water. It speaks or proclaims the message of a deity (1Sa 3:20; 1Ki 18:20; La 2:14).

- **Roeh** (seer) חֹזֶה (*hō·zě(h)*): Associated with discernment, the ability to see into people and situations, and to receive visions or dreams. One who receives and communicates a message from God, having the role of a prophet, possibly with some focus on the visual aspect of a communication from God (2Sa 24:11; 2Ki 17:13; 1Ch 21:9; 25:5; 29:29; 2Ch 9:29; 12:15; 19:2; 29:25, 30; 33:18; 35:15; Isa 29:10; 30:10; Am 7:12; Mic 3:7)

- **Shamar** (watchman) שָׁמַר (*šā·mǎr*): Those who discern God's timing and see when things will happen. **Keep**, i.e., cause a state or condition to remain (Job 2:6; Ps 17:4); be kept, set aside; **care for**, tend, keep, attend to, take care of an object, implying concern for the objects cared for (Hos 12:13)

- **Chozeh** (vision) חָזוֹן (*ḥā·zôn*): Those who enter into a trance and experience open visions. Revelation, i.e., communication from God to be communicated to others, with a focus on the visual aspects of the communication. (1 Sa 3:1; 1Ch 17:15; 2 Ch 32:32; Ps 89:20; Pr 29:18; Isa 1:1; 29:7; Jer 14:14; 23:16; La 2:9; Eze 7:13, 26; 12:22, 23, 24, 27; 13:16; Da 1:17; 8:1–11:14; Hos 12:11; Ob 1; Mic 3:6; Na 1:1; Hab 2:2).

- **Prophetes** (to foretell) προφήτης (*prophētēs*), ου (*ou*), ὁ (*ho*): Associated with future predictions. A proclaimer of God's utterances (Matt 1:22; Ac 21:10).

- **Nataph** (to preach) נָטַף (*nā·ṭǎp*): Known for tearing open heavens, bringing revelation, and delivering energetic, vocalized prophecies, often described as a burning fire. To ooze, i.e. distil gradually; by implication, to fall in drops; figuratively, to speak by inspiration (Job 29:22; Ezek 20:46; Ezek 21:2; Am 7:16).

Appointed

Being appointed means being assigned a task. Appointment comes with enough authority to accomplish the assigned task, as the appointment originates from someone with authority.

Appointment comes through faith, which is based on some degree of previous experience or evidence. The appointee believes in the authority that assigned the task. Appointment signifies *to tell, instruct, give direction, decree, give charge*, or *state with authority* what others must do. It can also mean to be forbidden, relating to what not to allow.

Anointed

Anointing comes through identity, usually through some degree of ceremony, such as the application of sacred oil on one's head, or taking an oath before witnesses, to acknowledge the grant of special authority and function (e.g. priest).

If a citizen of a community stops a robbery in a store, they would be considered a hero. Conversely, if a policeman did not attempt to stop a robbery in a store, they would be penalized since their authority was in their identity of being an officer of the law.

Despite being anointed as Israel's next King, David continued to perceive his identity as a shepherd boy, even after killing Goliath.[21] He had to mature into his anointing.

To prophesy is to speak into the chaos of the world to create order. As God's stewards on the Earth, we are tasked with representing his will as author. This means we first need to understand his will as it has been revealed throughout history. We need to know the patterns. We can come to that understanding through his Word.

What are some of the patterns we need to be aware of?

---

[21] Mast, D. L. (2015). *And David Perceived He Was King.* Xulon Press.

The first prophetic pattern

In the beginning, God created the heavens and the earth. *²The earth was without form and void, and darkness was over the face of the deep. And the Spirit of God was hovering over the face of the waters.* *³And God said,* - Genesis 1:1-3

b resit Elohim bara translates to English as *In the beginning, God created.*

The Hebrew *resit* (רֵאשִׁית *(rē(')·šît)*) is a reference to firstfruit, the first portion of something which has been set aside as a dedication and offering to God. The first word of Genesis is a reference to the firstfruit of God – Jesus.

While *resit* translates to *beginning* in English, its context encompasses the idea of *firstfruit*. Paul describes Jesus as *firstfruits* in 1 Corinthians 15:20.

> **8040** רֵאשִׁית *(rē(')·šît):* *n.; fem* ≡ *Str 7225; TWOT 2097e*—**1.** *LN 68.1–68.10* **what is first,** *the beginning, i.e., the initiation of an action, process, or state of being (Ps 111:10);* **2.** *LN 67.65–67.72* **the beginning,** *first of time, i.e., a point of time which is the beginning (non prior) in a duration (Ge 1:1);* **3.** *LN 65.20–65.29* **best,** *choice, i.e., that which is superior in value to all*

others in the same class or kind (Nu 24:20; Dt 33:21);
4. *LN 53.16–53.27* **firstfruit**, *i.e., the first portion of*
something which has been set aside in dedication and
offering to God (Ne 12:44; Pr 3:9), note: for focus on
the firstfruit as a food, see also domain LN 3.33–3.46[22]

God spoke into darkness and chaos to create order. *And God*
said, (said; אָמַר *('ā·mǎr)) signifies promise by declaration or*
command with intentional purpose.

The first task God gave Adam was to name every creature –
to speak order into chaos.

When Jesus stood before Pilate, he said, *For this reason was*
I born, for this purpose did I come into the world, to testify to
the truth. - John 18:37. To speak order into chaos. Our primary
assignment as God's imagers is to speak truth, order, into the
chaos of this world.

John declared in Revelation 19:10 that *The testimony of Jesus*
is the spirit of prophecy. Testimony represents communication
transmitted verbally or through behavior.

The Bible, God's word, testifies from its beginning to its
conclusion about the saving grace of Jesus. Our assignment,
should we accept it, is to speak God's order into chaos.

God instructed Adam directly to speak order into chaos by
naming every creature. The Bible does not indicate that God gave
that direct instruction to Eve. She had apparently been informed
about not eating from the tree of knowledge of good and evil,
as she repeated the command to the serpent – but added *neither*
shall you touch it, lest you die.

Adding to what God had instructed allowed the serpent to
twist God's words further, instilling doubt that led to pride.

---

[22] *Swanson, James. 1997. In Dictionary of Biblical Languages with Semantic Domains :*
Hebrew (Old Testament), electronic ed. Oak Harbor: Logos Research Systems, Inc.

Male

> ²⁷ *So God created man in his own image, in the image*
> *of God he created him; male and female he created*
> *them. - Genesis 2:27 (ESV)*

The Hebrew word *zakar* (זָכַר), translated as *male* in Genesis 2:27, means *remember* or *calling something to the forefront of your mind.* However, it often implies more than mere recollection; it's about focusing your attention so you can act. Males were created to remember God, and therefore, to remember God's ways. Men were created to pay attention to details – what they see, hear, and touch - to speak order where they discern chaos. We discern through the Word and the Spirit.

> ²⁴ *And God heard their groaning, and God*
> *remembered his covenant with Abraham, with Isaac,*
> *and with Jacob. – Exodus 2:24 (ESV)*

When God heard the groans of his people in Egypt, he *zakars* his covenant with Abraham and takes action.

In the context of the Sabbath, it signifies both remembering God's creation on the seventh day and keeping it holy by ceasing from work and engaging in activities like study, prayer, and family time. The commandment to *remember the Sabbath day, to keep it holy* (Exodus 20:10) emphasizes both the intellectual recall and the practical affirmation of the Sabbath's significance.

David and Asaph often wrote songs celebrating the benefits of remembering God.

> *I will remember (zakar) the deeds of the Lord. -*
> *Psalm 77:11*

Some portions of Old Testament text can be challenging to read simply due to lengthy lists of genealogical lineage. Occasional breaks in the text remind us to pay attention to what makes these sections unique.

Jabez

In the midst of chronicling Judah's descendants, the monotony of who begot whom shifts, and we recognize something special in the description of Jabez as *more honorable.*

> *⁹ Jabez was more honorable than his brothers; and his mother called his name Jabez, saying, "Because I bore him in pain." ¹⁰ Jabez called upon the God of Israel, saying, "Oh that you would bless me and enlarge my border, and that your hand might be with me, and that you would keep me from harm so that it might not bring me pain!" – 1 Chronicles 4:9-10 (ESV)*

Jabez's name means *born in pain.* We can imagine the taunting he faced while growing up. In those days, a person's name and land ownership were of utmost importance. Jabez is remembered for calling out to God, asking to be blessed (favored, honored). The word *harm* is translated from the Hebrew רע (*rǎʿ*), which actually means *evil* – that which is not of God. He clearly sought to *zakar* God. Jabez's prayer mirrors the same pattern of the prayer Jesus taught his disciples, known as The Lord's Prayer: *lead me not into temptation.*

God remembered Jabez because Jabez remembered God.

Asher

Asher was the eighth son of Jacob. While the other sons of Jacob list their descendants and lands they were allotted, Asher's lineage begins similarly, but concludes with a noteworthy addition.

> [40] *All of these were men of Asher, heads of fathers' houses, approved, mighty warriors, chiefs of the princes. Their number enrolled by genealogies, for service in war, was 26,000 men.* - *1 Chronicles 7:40 (ESV)*

What kind of man was Asher that 26,000 of his descendants were *heads of fathers' houses, approved, mighty warriors, chiefs of the princes.*? For a more in-depth discussion of Asher, read *The Warrior Within* by Pat Williams.

David

During the time David was fleeing from Saul, he and his men served the Philistine ruler of Gath. David even agreed to fight alongside Achish against Saul's (Israel's) army. When the other Philistine rulers objected, Achish sent David back to the town where he and his men lived, Ziklag.

Upon arriving at Ziklag, David and his men found the town burned, their families and livestock taken. David's men threatened to stone him. In response, David called for the priest Abiathar to consult God. But before consulting, the last sentence in 1 Samuel 30:6 tells us:

> *But David strengthened himself in the Lord his God (ESV)*

David first drew strength from the Lord by remembering what God had done for him. This is a pattern we would do well to follow – to *zakar* what God has accomplished in our lives.

Female

The Hebrew word *ezer*, translated as *helper* in Genesis, means *one to assist, strength or power to accomplish a task*, or *rescuer*. There seems to be some resistance these days regarding the term *helper* or *assistant*. It's important to recognize that Eve was created from Adam, indicating their equal creation. They shared the same DNA.

> **6469** *I.* עֵזֶר *('ē·zĕr): n.masc,;* ≡ *Str 5828; TWOT 1598a*—**1.** *LN 35.1–35.18* **helper,** *assistant, i.e., one who assists and serves another with what is needed (Ge 2:18, 20; Ex 18:4; Dt 33:29; Eze 12:14; Hos 13:9);* **2.** *LN 35.1–35.18* **help,** *assistance, i.e., acts of supplying what is needed to another (Dt 33:7, 26; Ps 20:3[EB 2]; 33:20; 70:6[EB 5]; 115:9, 10, 11; 121:1, 2; 124:8; 146:5; Isa 30:5; Da 11:34);* **3.** *LN 76* **strength,** *formally, help, i.e., power to accomplish a task (Ps 89:20[EB 19]), note: some change text to 5694 or 5694.5, note: for another interp see next;* **4.** *LN 9.24–9.33* **boy,** *lad, i.e., a young person of relatively little power compared to a great warrior (Ps 89:20[EB 19]), note: this meaning based on Ugaritic analogy, see WBC 20:410*[23]

The King James Version uses *help meet*, instead of *helper*. The term *meet* is translated from the Hebrew *kenedgo*, which means *facing*, *in front of*, or *face-to-face*. A face-to-face relationship implies two distinct individuals created equally.

The Hebrew word *ezer* (or its forms) appears twenty-three times in the Old Testament.

The first two references are to Eve.

Six times it refers to powerful nations around Israel.

The remaining fifteen instances reference God as our help. This context of the word *ezer* confirms the idea of *strength or power to accomplish a task*, or *rescuer* context. It signifies providing strength where others are weak and emphasizes unity.

---

[23] Swanson, James. 1997. In *Dictionary of Biblical Languages with Semantic Domains : Hebrew (Old Testament)*, electronic ed. Oak Harbor: Logos Research Systems, Inc.

Beyond Eve, numerous women in Scripture exemplify the pattern of *ezer*. Some of them include:

Midwives

The Hebrew population enslaved in Egypt grew to a point that the Egyptians felt threatened. Pharaoh's solution was to instruct midwives to kill Hebrew male infants at birth.

However, the midwives who defied this order acted according to their conscience, respecting God's creation.

Ruth

Ruth's unwavering loyalty, strong character, and willingness to support Naomi demonstrate her role as an *ezer*, a true partner and helper in Naomi's life. The name Naomi means *pleasant*. When she and Ruth travelled to Bethlehem from Moab, Naomi told her friends to call her *mara*, which means *bitter*.

Without a husband, at an advanced age, and having lost both of her sons, Naomi felt that God's hand was against her. Yet God was working through Ruth to redeem Naomi's family and comfort her.

Ruth embodies a Proverbs 31 woman or *ezer*; toiling, harvesting, serving, gracious, generous, and industrious.

The book of Ruth reveals a pattern of God's hesed love, directly from God and through people. Ruth, a Gentile, was chosen by God to announce his gathering the people disinherited at Babel back to himself.

Abigail

Nabal was a wealthy man. When David sent some men to request food Nabal refused and cursed David. Enraged, David set out with some of his men to kill Nabal. Abigail, one of Nabal's wives, learned of Nabal's action, gathered servants and provision, and went to intercept David. She bowed before him and pointed out her husband was a fool. She also told David he had kingship written all over him and continued to compliment him. David reconsidered his plan to kill Nabal because Abagail spoke to the king within him. Shortly after, Nabal died, and Abigail eventually became one of David's wives.

Every man possesses two natures – a king and a fool. The one you address is the one that responds. The best friend you have is the one that speaks to the king in you when the fool in you is speaking.

A man doesn't marry a woman because of how she looks; he marries her because of how he feels in her presence.

Esther

Although Esther initially came to the king's palace to be trained as a submissive harem girl, she found the inner strength to advocate for the sake of her people. She took significant risks to persuade the king to issue a decree allowing Jews to defend themselves.

As queen, Esther is seen as an *ezer* to her people, using her influence to redeem them and bring order to chaos.

It's in the name

What does God want? He desires family.[24]

If we are truly family, we share certain traits. Scripture tells us that God possesses many attributes and has shared some with us. While we are not omniscient, omnipotent, or omnipresent, we do have free will.[25]

Prophecy, speaking divine utterance, consistently presents a pattern of choice, often expressed as behold or beware.

---

[24] Heiser, M. S. (2018). *What Does God Want?* Blind Spot Press.

[25] Tozer, A. W., & Fessenden, D. E. (2015). *The Attributes of God. Volume 2, Deeper into the Father's heart.* Moody Publishers.

The forgotten missions of Jesus

A sk most people, including many Christians, where mankind went wrong, and they would likely cite Adam and Eve's sin in the Garden of Eden – the Fall.

If we were to ask ancient Israelites the same question, they would likely point to three rebellions against God: The Fall, The Watchers (Genesis 6), and The Tower of Babel (Genesis 11).

Jesus didn't come into our world solely to redeem us from the sin that occurred during The Fall. He came to redeem all three rebellions: The Fall, The Watchers, and The Tower of Babel. Each of these rebellions was instigated by members of God's heavenly council. As Paul wrote in his letter to the church at Ephesus:

> *12 For we do not wrestle against flesh and blood, but against the rulers, against the authorities, against the cosmic powers over this present darkness, against the spiritual forces of evil in the heavenly places. - Ephesians 6:12 (ESV)*

The Fall

Deception is worse than temptation and accusation.[26] Deception can lead to both temptation and accusation.

---

[26] Anderson, N. T. (2019). *The Bondage Breaker.* Harvest House Publishers.

We can fairly easily discern when we're being tempted or accused. However, when we don't know the truth, we can be deceived because we aren't able to discern the choices before us. We need circuitry, the logic, in place to make binary decisions that either open or close doors, guiding us toward the best outcome.

Eve was deceived. Adam was silent.

The Watchers

Authority over the Earth had been transferred through deceptive tactics, leaving mankind struggling with a loss of identity and a struggle to remember God.

Genesis 6 provides a brief description of the sons of God mating with human women, which was a breach of the boundary God had set between heaven and earth.

> *6 ¹ When man began to multiply on the face of the land and daughters were born to them, ² the sons of God saw that the daughters of man were attractive. And they took as their wives any they chose. –*
> *Genesis 6:1-2 (ESV)*

The brevity of Genesis 6:1–4, combined with the unfamiliarity of concepts outside our physical experience, invites multiple interpretations. The phrase *sons of God* (בְּנֵי-הָאֱלֹהִים, *b'nei ha-Elohim*) appears elsewhere in the Old Testament, notably in Job, offering clues but no definitive answers. The *daughters of mankind* (בְּנוֹת הָאָדָם, *b'not ha-adam*) and the resulting offspring, often linked to the Nephilim, add further complexity.

The Hebrew word *elohim* refers to spiritual beings rather than human beings. Some Bible translations use *sons of Israel* instead of *sons of God*. However, Israel did not exist at the time Genesis 6 was written, and *b'nei ha-Elohim* appears in other Old

Testament passages that clearly refer to angels in Heaven. For example, passages like Psalm 82, where God (*Elohim*) presides over a council of *gods* (*elohim*) as well as Job 1:6, 2:1, and 38:7, where the *sons of God* participate in heavenly assemblies.

1 Enoch contains much more detail on the Genesis 6 text, even naming the captains of two hundred fallen *elohim* who made a pact. One of those captains was named Azazel. We find that name in Leviticus 16, which describes Day of Atonement activity with two goats – one as sacrificed to Yahweh, and one sent into the wilderness carrying the sins of the people as the *scapegoat* for Azazel.

Genesis 6:14 informs us that the result of the rebellion was the Nephilim, giant offspring. Because of the violence that ensued, God decided to start over through Noah.

> *⁹ These are the generations of Noah. Noah was a righteous man, blameless in his generation. Noah walked with God - Genesis 6:9 (ESV)*

The waters receded from the earth on Tishri 1 (the first month, first day of the month).

> *¹³ In the six hundred and first year, in the first month, the first day of the month, the waters were dried from off the earth. – Genesis 8:13 (ESV)*

This followed the same pattern on the same calendar day that Creation recorded.

> *⁹ And God said, "Let the waters under the heavens be gathered together into one place, and let the dry land appear." And it was so. ¹⁰ God called the dry land Earth, and the waters that were gathered together he called Seas. And God saw that it was good - Genesis 1:9-10 (ESV)*

God gave Noah and his sons the same set of instructions – the Edenic covenant – that he had given to Adam and Eve: to be fruitful, multiply, and fill the earth.

> **9** *¹ And God blessed Noah and his sons and said to them, "Be fruitful and multiply and fill the earth. ² The fear of you and the dread of you shall be upon every beast of the earth and upon every bird of the heavens, upon everything that creeps on the ground and all the fish of the sea. Into your hand they are delivered. – Genesis 9:1-2 (ESV)*

Does the term *sons of God* in Genesis 6 conflict with the reference to Jesus in John 3:16 as the *only begotten son*?

The English *only begotten* is translated from the Greek μονογενής (monogenēs). *Monogenes* actually means *unique*, or *one of a kind*. There was none other like Jesus.

Isaac is also described as *monogenes* in Hebrews 11:17. Isaac was not Abraham's first or only son; Ishmael was Abraham's first-born son. Isaac is referred to as *monogenes* because he was unique, the son of God's covenant with Abraham and Sarah.

> **3666** *μονογενής (monogenēs), ές (es): adj.; ≡ Str 3439; TDNT 4.737—LN 58.52* **unique**, *only, one and only, i.e.,, one of a kind: (many versions) only begotten (Lk 7:12; 8:42; 9:38; Jn 1:14, 18; 3:16, 18; Heb 11:17; 1Jn 4:9; Jn 1:34 v.r.)*[27]

---

[27] Swanson, James. 1997. In *Dictionary of Biblical Languages with Semantic Domains: Greek (New Testament)*, electronic ed. Oak Harbor: Logos Research Systems, Inc.

The Tower

God instructed Noah and his sons to fill the earth – to spread out. Instead, they chose to congregate. The description of the third rebellion begins in Genesis 11.

> *⁴ Then they said, "Come, let us build ourselves a city and a tower with its top in the heavens, and let us make a name for ourselves, lest we be dispersed over the face of the whole earth." – Genesis 11:4 (ESV)*

While translations typically refer to what was being built as a tower, it was specifically a structure known as a ziggurat, intended to house a deity.

Ziggurat. Term meaning "temple tower"; a ziggurat was similar in profile to the step pyramid of Egypt and was used for worship. They were frequent in the major cities of Mesopotamia. The Tower of Babel (Gn 11:1–9) is believed to be of this construction. It was widely believed that deities dwelt above, in high places. Therefore worship was more appropriate on hills or mountains. There are no hills in Mesopotamia, nor is there building stone. Consequently the inhabitants built with mud brick. The ziggurats of mud brick were constructed as substitutes for hills, where the worshiper or priest could get closer to the gods. Like the pyramids of Egypt, these temple towers were four square. Instead of having sloping sides, there was a succession of terraces, each smaller than the one below. Access to each level was by stairways or ramps. The shrine or altar was on top, where the priests would officiate at sacrifices, incantations, and prayers. The great seven-story ziggurat at Babylon measured nearly 300 square feet at the base and rose to about the same height.[28]

---

[28] Elwell, Walter A., and Barry J. Beitzel. 1988. "Ziggurat." In *Baker Encyclopedia of the Bible*, 2:2198. Grand Rapids, MI: Baker Book House.

God confused their languages so they could not communicate effectively to continue their project.

A pattern of 70

The people dispersed, and God assigned *bene ha Elohim* (sons of God) to govern each of them according to God's covenant. Genesis 10 identifies 70 nations among the people dispersed at Babel. We see the pattern of 70 repeated throughout the Bible.

Seventy descendants of Jacob went to Egypt after Joseph revealed himself to his brothers and then sent for his father Jacob.

God instructed Moses to call 70 elders to the Tent of Meeting so that he could place his spirit upon them. Once that took place, the 70 began to prophesy.

> *24 So Moses went out and told the people the words of the Lord. And he gathered seventy men of the elders of the people and placed them around the tent. 25 Then the Lord came down in the cloud and spoke to him, and took some of the Spirit that was on him and put it on the seventy elders. And as soon as the Spirit rested on them, they prophesied. But they did not continue doing it.*
>
> *26 Now two men remained in the camp, one named Eldad, and the other named Medad, and the Spirit rested on them. They were among those registered, but they had not gone out to the tent, and so they prophesied in the camp. – Numbers 11:24-26 (ESV)*

The Hebrews were captives in Babylon for 70 years before they were allowed to return to the Promised Land.

Jesus sent 70 disciples to spread the Gospel (Luke 10). Most translations render the Greek ἑβδομήκοντα (hebdomēkonta) δισμυριάς (dismyrias)[29] as 72. ἑβδομήκοντα (hebdomēkonta) does translate as 70. δισμυριάς (dismyrias) refers to *doubling* and means and can imply *as pairs.*

After being appointed as Apostle to the Gentiles, Paul's ministry is recorded as extending to 70 nations.

In Hebrew, the number 70, represented by the letter *ayin* derives from two perfect numbers: seven (representing perfection) and ten (representing completeness and God's law). Thus, it symbolizes perfect spiritual order, carried out. It can also represent a period of judgment.

Abraham and Sarah

God called Abram and Sarai out of Ur of the Chaldeans as his inheritance – starting over again. The pattern of the Edenic covenant was essentially repeated when God promised Abram and Sarai that their descendants would become a great nation - be fruitful and multiply.

Observe that Abram's and Sarai's names were changed by adding the letter *hey* (ה; *h*) to become Abraham and Sarah. The Hebrew letter *hey* signifies *breath, air, known identity.* God was breathing life into them, as he did with Adam and Eve, to create a new beginning.

What does God require of us?

> [8] *He has told you, O man, what is good; and what does the Lord require of you but to do justice, and to love kindness, and to walk humbly with your God? - Micah 6:8 (ESV)*

Thomas Edison lived in Fort Myers, Florida, where he often worked in a lab on his property. He constantly had graduate

---

[29] Swanson, James. 1997. In *Dictionary of Biblical Languages with Semantic Domains: Greek (New Testament)*, electronic ed. Oak Harbor: Logos Research Systems, Inc.

students assisting in his creative endeavors, and members of the press were eager to report on Edison's efforts.

On the day Edison was to create the first light bulb, many people were in the lab. The staff created the filament, the glass bulb, and the base to conduct electricity from the bulb socket. The final step was to join the glass bulb to the combined base and filament component using a vacuum machine located in the upstairs loft.

When it was time for the vacuum machine's final step, Edison handed the components to a graduate student to take upstairs. The young man caught his toe on the lip of the top step, dropped the components as he fell to the floor, and the components shattered.

Since the entire process took an entire day, Edison and his team debated whether to repeat the steps immediately, or get some sleep before continuing. They agreed to try again.

When it was time for the vacuum machine, Edison handed the components to the same young man he had entrusted the first time. As the young man moved out of sight at the top of the stairs, a reporter approached Edison and asked why he would trust the same young man with the components after the first attempt ended in failure. Edison's replied, *There is more at stake here than the electric light bulb.* Edison demonstrated humility by valuing the young man's integrity over the assembly of the first light bulb.[30]

The pattern is documented

Except for the books of Luke and Acts, every book of the Bible was written by an ancient Israelite. Texts do not have to be canonical to be important. Do not hesitate to read ancient Israelite texts outside the Bible, as this will deepen your understanding of

[30] Newton, J. D. (1989). *Uncommon friends : life with Thomas Edison, Henry Ford, Harvey Firestone, Alexis Carrel, & Charles Lindbergh.* Harcourt Brace Jovanovich.

how the author of the Bible thought. For instance, Peter, Jude, and Jesus cited ancient texts (e.g., 1 Enoch). *Dictionary of Deities and Demons in the Bible* (Greenfield) is a good reference.

Hebrew is the only language that is phonetic (sound), numeric, and pictographic, providing it with more context than other languages that may present only two of those attributes. Originally, it consisted of twenty-three consonants. Vowels were not added to Hebrew until around 800 AD. The choice of vowels can add or change the context of a word.

Each Hebrew word has a numeric value, derived from the sum of the value of its letters. Patterns of the same number appearing throughout the Hebrew text connect passages, indicating prophetic significance. The Hebrew alphabet consists of 22 letters; the first is *aleph*, representing the number one, and the last is *tav*, representing the number 400.

We live in a universe based on math and quantum physics, and Genesis 1 reveals how letters (with numerical value) are the building blocks of creation. Consequently, the spiritual code to creation surrounds us daily, waiting for us to discover its greatest depths.

For example, the Hebrew word *echad* translates to the English word *one*. *Echad* is spelled a*leph* (1), *het* (8), *dalet* (4). $1 + 8 + 4 = 13$. The Hebrew number thirteen symbolizes oneness. While Western culture often views thirteen as unlucky, biblically, it signifies spiritual blessing.

The Bible reveals God's intended patterns in our lives. Let's explore some of these revelations embedded in the language or culture.

Interesting patterns

The Old Testament

Genesis 1 through 11 appears to establish a pattern that recurs throughout the remainder of the Bible.

God provided a pattern for Adam and Eve, which is repeated with Noah, then repeated with Abraham, and again through Moses. We have been given multiple chances.

The New Testament

Other than the books of Luke and Acts, all of the Bible was written by ancient Israelite authors. Aside from Luke, the authors of the New Testament were raised learning from the Torah. Much of what Luke wrote was derived from what he learned from Paul. Many biblical scholars have referred to the New Testament as a commentary on the Old Testament.

The community at Qumran, where the Dead Sea Scrolls were discovered in 1948, was a very conservative group of Jews who viewed the Pharisees and Sadducees as extreme liberals of Judaism. The Qumran community expected the Messiah during the period of time when Jesus conducted his ministry. They likely experienced confusion as they also sought a military leader to revive Israel from Roman rule.

Michael Ferguson

Generations

The Hebrew word *toledot* translates to English as *generations* or *genealogies.*

The word *toledot* occurs 39 times in the Old Testament. The significance of God's plan (prophecy) regarding generations lies in the detail of the word – its letters. The first occurrence in Genesis 2:4, is spelled with six letters (right to left): *tav-vav-lamed-dalet-vav-tav.* The Hebrew letter *vav* is a pictograph of a hook or nail. When *vav* is situated between two other characters, it indicates conjunction – *and.*

These are the generations of heavens and the earth when they were created, in the day that the LORD God made earth and heaven. – Genesis 2:4

> *generations:* תּוֹלְדֹת
> *tav: (ת) - covenant*
> *vav: (ו) – nail*
> *lamed: (ל) – shepherd*
> *dalet: (ד) – open tent door*
> *vav: (ו) - nail*
> *tav: (ת) covenant*

The literal meaning of *toledot* can be expressed as: *The shepherd is connected to the covenant through an open door.*

Genesis 3 records the fall of man (the shepherd) through sin. The next instance of *toledot* occurs in Genesis 5:1.

> *This is the book of the generations of Adam. In the day when God created man, He made him in the likeness of God. He created them male and female, and He blessed them and named them Man in the day when they were created. -* Genesis 5:1-2

This instance of *toledot* (Genesis 5:1) is missing the second vav תּוֹלְלָת. The open tent door no longer connects the shepherd to the covenant.

In the remaining 37 instances of *toledot* the spelling is either missing one or both of the vavs, except for the instance in Ruth 4:18, where the word contains both of the vavs, as it does in the first instance of Genesis 2:4.

And YHWH enabled her to conceive, and she gave birth to a son. Then the women said to Naomi, "Blessed is YHWH who has not left you without a redeemer today, and may his name become famous in Israel. May he also be to you a restorer of life and a sustainer of your old age; for your daughter-in-law, who loves you and is better to you than seven sons, has given birth to him..."

...Now these are the generations of Perez: to Perez was born Hezron and to Hezron was born Ram, and to Ram, Amminadab, and to Amminadab was born Nahshon, and to Nahshon, Salmon, and to Salmon was born Boaz, and to Boaz, Obed, and to Obed was born Jesse, and to Jesse, David. - Ruth 14:13b-15, 18

The generations (*toledot*) now signify reconnection to the covenant through Perez (a son of Judah) to Obed and leading to David. Given that Scripture is inspired by God, this is not a coincidence; it serves as testimony and prophecy of Jesus. Ruth was a Moabite (Gentile), and Boaz was a direct descendant of Abraham. The covenant was restored through Abraham for all of mankind. Ruth's Gentile background signifies the beginning of the gathering of all nations through God's promise to Abraham.

The Ark of the Covenant

Exodus describes the craftsmanship of Bezalel in creating the elements of the Tent of Meeting, altar, lampstands, bowls, and the Ark of the Covenant. It details the materials, dimensions, and design of these objects. This section of Scripture is lengthy and easy to overlook while seeking the narrative about the people's actions. However, it contains significant prophetic insights.

Exodus 37:7 describes the construction of the Mercy Seat atop the Ark of the Covenant, with an angel at each end, where the blood of the sacrificial lamb would be sprinkled each year on the Day of Atonement.

> *⁷ And he made two cherubim of gold. He made them of hammered work on the two ends of the mercy seat, ⁸ one cherub on the one end, and one cherub on the other end. – Exodus 37:7*

Jewish tradition emphasizes that the high priest would tremble before the presence of God and whisper the name YHWH (*yod-hey-vav-hey*) with reverence and fear. It is pronounced as *Yahweh*, or *Jehovah*. The name can also be translated as a phrase. *yod* represents a *hand*. *hey* means *behold*. *vav* can signifies a *nail* or *spike*, and *hey* again means *behold*. God's name whispered as the lamb's blood was sprinkled on the Mercy Seat annually on the Day of Atonement can be interpreted as:

> *behold the hand, behold the nail*

It was a prophetic testimony of Jesus' sacrificial atonement for our sins.

The description in John 20:12 recounts what Mary Magdelene encountered when she stooped back into Jesus' tomb after Peter and John had left.

¹² And she saw two angels in white, sitting where the body of Jesus had lain, one at the head and one at the feet. – John 20:12

The image that Mary perceived reflects the Mercy Seat that Bezalel created to crown the Ark of the Covenant.

Day of Entry

Passover. In Hebrew tradition, the Day of Entry was first observed in Egypt when God instructed the Israelites through Moses to take a one-year old lamb without blemish into their homes, keep it for four days, prepare the lamb for a meal, and brush its blood on their doorpost and lintel

Promised Land. The Hebrews crossed the Jordan into the Promised Land on the Day of Entry forty years later. Four days later, they celebrated Passover in the Promised Land.

Anointed One. Daniel proclaims arrival of *an anointed one, a prince* calculated *from the going out of the word to restore and build Jerusalem*. The King James translation uses *The Messiah, The Prince.*

²⁵ Know therefore and understand that from the going out of the word to restore and build Jerusalem to the coming of an anointed one, a prince, there shall be seven weeks. Then for sixty-two weeks it shall be built again with squares and moat, but in a troubled time. ²⁶ And after the sixty-two weeks, an anointed one shall be cut off and shall have nothing. – Daniel 9:25-26 (ESV)

In ancient Hebrew, *weeks* had multiple meanings, which scholars can discern from context. The context in the Daniel passage indicates that *weeks* means *seven units,* with *units* usually understood as *years*. Using this definition, we can calculate when the Messiah will arrive: $(7 \times 7) + (62 \times 7) = 49 + 434 = 483$ years.

The prophecy tells us: *from the time the word goes out to restore and rebuild Jerusalem*. So, who issued this decree, and when? Several possibilities exist, but the decree to restore Jerusalem was made by the Persian king Artaxerxes to Nehemiah on March 5, 444 BC (Nehemiah 2:1–8).[31]

A solar year has 365 days, 5 hours, 48 minutes, and 46 seconds, or 365.2422 days. The Hebrew calendar is based on lunar cycles with a lunar year consisting of exactly 360 days (12 months of 30 days).

There are 173,880 days in 483 lunar years: $360 \times 483 = 173{,}880$ days.

There are 476.068 solar years in 173,880 days: $173{,}880 \div 365.2422 = 476.068$ years.

Converting the decimal part (0.068) to days ($0.068 \times 365.2422 = 24.8$ days), the prophesied time for the Messiah to arrive amounts to be 476 years and 25 days.

Adding 476 years and 25 days to March 5, 444 BC - the date on which the decree to rebuild Jerusalem was issued - brings us to March 30, AD 33, the day when Jesus entered Jerusalem riding a colt. On the Hebrew calendar, this was the Day of Entry.

Esther

Most of March coincides with the Hebrew month of Adar. The one Hebrew holiday in Adar is the Feast of Purim, which celebrates God's deliverance of the Hebrews in Babylon from Haman's evil plot of annihilation. While the feast spans two days on the calendar, it permeates the entire month of Adar, honoring God's divine intervention in rescuing his people.

---

[31] Hoehner, H. W. (1981). *Chronological Aspects of the Life of Christ*. Zondervan.

The book of Esther was not readily accepted as Canon (part of divinely inspired text) because it does not contain a direct reference to God, or his name.

About 49,000 Jews returned to the Promised Land after the decree of Cyrus allowed them to return and rebuild the temple. Many Jews chose to remain in Babylon, having settled into homes, business, raising families, and were prospering. God was visibly active with the remnant that returned to Jerusalem, while his presence was not evident to the Jews who remained in Babylon. Some scholars believe this is a reference to Deuteronomy 31:16-18, wherein God reminds Moses of Israel's disobedience when instructed to enter the promised land: *At that time I will hide my face from them on account of all the evil they commit by worshiping other gods.*

However, God's name does appear in Esther as acrostics. An acrostic is defined as *a poem, word puzzle, or other composition in which certain letters in each line form a word or words.* Psalm 119 is one of the best known examples of acrostics. Its 176 verses are divided into 22 stanzas of eight verses each, with each stanza beginning with a successive letter of the Hebrew alphabet.

God's name is present forwards and backwards in Esther. It appears twice forwards when spoken by Israelites and twice backwards when spoken by Gentiles. God was watching over and blessing his people even though the story does not seem to focus on him. He may have hidden his face, but did not forget his people.[32]

> **20** *So when the decree made by the king is proclaimed throughout all his kingdom, for it is vast, all women will give honor to their husbands, high and low alike. – Esther 1:20 (ESV), spoken by Memucan (a Gentile).*

Note: *Hebrew is read from right to left.*

---

[32] Bullinger, E. W. (1999). *The Name of Jehovah in the Book of Esther.* Open Bible Trust ; New Berlin, Wis.

all the women will give **H**i' Vekal **H**annashim **Y**ittenu
(HVHY)

⁴ *And Esther said, "If it please the king, let the
king and Haman come today to a feast that I have
prepared for the king." - Esther 5:4, spoken by Esther*

let the king and Haman come today **Y**abo' **H**ammelek
V Haman **H**ayyom (YHVH)

¹³ *Yet all this is worth nothing to me, so long as I
see Mordecai the Jew sitting at the king's gate. -
Esther 5:13 spoken by Haman (a Gentile)*

*this is worth nothing to me ze***H** eynenn**V** shove**H** l**Y**
(HVHY)

⁷ *And the king arose in his wrath from the wine-
drinking and went into the palace garden, but Haman
stayed to beg for his life from Queen Esther, for he saw
that harm was determined against him by the king. -
Esther 7:7 written by author of the book of Esther*

that evil was determined against him k**Y** kalthа**H**
elay**V** hara'a**H** (YHVH)

There is a fifth acrostic. When King Ahasuerus demands to
know who would conspire against the life of the Queen - Esther.

⁵ *Then King Ahasuerus said to Queen Esther, "Who
is he, and where is he, who has dared to do this?*

who is he, and where is he, who has dared to do this
hu'**E** ze**H** ve**Y** ze**H** (EHYH)

EHYH translates to I AM, which is a reference to God. Who
could put those words in Ahasuerus' mouth to proclaim God's
protection of Esther and her people?

We are greatly favored even when things may not seem to be going the way we expected or wanted. These are divine utterances informing us that God is watching over us even when we don't perceive his presence.

Sower of seed

> *⁴ And when a great crowd was gathering and people from town after town came to him, he said in a parable, ⁵ "A sower went out to sow his seed. And as he sowed, some fell along the path and was trampled underfoot, and the birds of the air devoured it. ⁶ And some fell on the rock, and as it grew up, it withered away, because it had no moisture. ⁷ And some fell among thorns, and the thorns grew up with it and choked it. ⁸ And some fell into good soil and grew and yielded a hundredfold." – Luke 8:5-8 (ESV)*

There is an interesting embedded pattern in the parable of the sower of seed.

Anyone who has been around farming knows that the first thing a sower of seed does is obtain the best seed possible. Before they sow, they invest a lot of time and effort in preparing the tools and the soil to receive the seed.

Notice what the parable doesn't tell us. The sower didn't stop, or go back to pick up the seed that fell along the path. The sower didn't chase the birds away from devouring the seed. The sower didn't expend effort to retrieve the seed that feel on the rock, or among thorns. The sower kept sowing, knowing that the seed that fell into good soil would yield a bountiful harvest.

Jesus' birth

After Daniel told Nebuchadnezzar his dream and interpreted it, Nebuchadnezzar came off his throne and bowed to Daniel, acknowledging that Daniel's God was above all others. Nebuchadnezzar then made Daniel chief over all the Magi in Babylon. In other words, Daniel was now in a position to teach and train the Magi.

Just as God had placed Joseph in Egypt, God placed Daniel in Babylon.

It doesn't seem far-fetched to wonder whether God placed Daniel there to train the Magi to look for a star that would announce the birth of the King of the Jews – Jesus.

They had the countdown from Daniel, and they knew what to look for in the skies. They had an understanding of the stars, the word of God, and prophecy,

The Dead Sea Scrolls calendar, Jesuss by the community at Qumran is the only calendar in the ancient world that creates a time window for the Messiah's arrival that matches Jesus.[33]

Paul asks in Romans 10:14 whether people can believe if they have not heard the Gospel.

> *[14] How then will they call on him in whom they have not believed? And how are they to believe in him of whom they have never heard? ..... [17] So faith comes from hearing, and hearing through the word of Christ. – Romans 10:14, 17*

Paul answers the question in verse 18 by quoting Psalm 19:4. Was Paul referencing what the Magi had been watching for in the skies?

---

[33] *What Do The Magi and The Dead Sea Scrolls Have In Common?*; Dr. Michael S. Heiser; https://www.youtube.com/watch?v=52hVgs5ykFc

[18] But I ask, have they not heard? Indeed they have, for "Their voice has gone out to all the earth, and their words to the ends of the world." - Psalm 19:4 (ESV)

Using NASA technology to study the skies around the time of Jesus' birth, Rick Larson discovered an extremely rare triple conjunction: The *king* star (Regulus) crossing the *king* planet (Jupiter) within the constellation of the lion (Leo), *king* of the animals, three times.[34] King, king, king. Moreover, the constellation of the lion, which is called that in every language as far back as records go, has an association with the kingly tribe of Judah - the lion of Judah. The message was all there.

Plugging the data from Revelation 12 into an astronomy app reveals an eighty-minute window of time for Jesus' birth that would correspond to September 11, 3 B.C on what we use as the Gregorian calendar. That date was Tishri 1, the first day of the Hebrew calendar, the first day of creation, Noah's birthday, and the day the floodwaters receded to allow Noah and his family to exit the Ark, which was also used as the first day of reign for every Davidic king.

Jesus was born on the same calendar day that Creation occurred.

Prayer that's always answered

The first mention of Jesus in the Bible after his birth occurs when he was twelve years old. His family traveled to Jerusalem to participate in celebration of Passover. The record tells us that Joseph and Mary realized Jesus was not in the group they were traveling back home with. They returned to Jerusalem and searched for three days before finding Jesus in the Temple.

---

[34] *The Star of Bethlehem – Exploring the evidence about the star that marked history.* (n.d.). https://bethlehemstar.com/

After Mary told Jesus they had searched for him, he asked: *Why were you searching for me? Didn't you know I would be in my Father's house?* At this early age, Jesus' focus was on glorifying and honoring God.

This passage poses questions to us as it did to Joseph and Mary. Are we focused more on our destination than our devotion? Do we know Jesus as well as we claim to? When God asks us a question, it isn't so God can understand something about us; it is so we can understand something about God.

Jesus is in the place we left him in after the decision we made without him. We won't receive the peace we're looking for until we return to Jesus.

John 17 records what is known as the High Priestly Prayer, which patterns what is described above about Jesus at twelve. It's Jesus' prayers in Gethsemane the night before he was crucified. It reveals prayer that will always be answered.

> *Father, the hour has come; glorify your Son that the Son may glorify you, ² since you have given him authority over all flesh, to give eternal life to all whom you have given him. ³ And this is eternal life, that they know you, the only true God, and Jesus Christ whom you have sent. ⁴ I glorified you on earth, having accomplished the work that you gave me to do. ⁵ And now, Father, glorify me in your own presence with the glory that I had with you before the world existed. – John 17:1-5 (ESV)*

Once again, Jesus repeats the pattern that has been revealed throughout his life – to glorify and honor the Father. This is prayer that is always answered because it seeks what Jesus seeks.

We see this pattern in Daniel's prayer once he realized the seventy years of bondage Jeremiah prophesied were about to be completed. Daniel didn't wait to see if it happened; he prayed – fervently.

> **9** *¹ In the first year of Darius the son of Ahasuerus, by descent a Mede, who was made king over the realm of the Chaldeans— ² in the first year of his reign, I, Daniel, perceived in the books the number of years that, according to the word of the Lord to Jeremiah the prophet, must pass before the end of the desolations of Jerusalem, namely, seventy years.*
>
> *³ Then I turned my face to the Lord God, seeking him by prayer and pleas for mercy with fasting and sackcloth and ashes. – Daniel 9:1-3 (ESV)*

What did he petition?

> *¹⁶ "O Lord, according to all your righteous acts, let your anger and your wrath turn away from your city Jerusalem, your holy hill, because for our sins, and for the iniquities of our fathers, Jerusalem and your people have become a byword among all who are around us. ¹⁷ Now therefore, O our God, listen to the prayer of your servant and to his pleas for mercy, and for your own sake, O Lord, make your face to shine upon your sanctuary, which is desolate. ¹⁸ O my God, incline your ear and hear. Open your eyes and see our desolations, and the city that is called by your name. For we do not present our pleas before you because of our righteousness, but because of your great mercy. ¹⁹ O Lord, hear; O Lord, forgive. O Lord, pay attention and act. Delay not, for your own sake, O my God, because your city and your people are called by your name." - Daniel 9:16-19 (ESV)*

- Glorify God in his righteousness
- Repentance
- Listen
- Favor
- Hear
- Mercy
- Forgiveness
- Do not delay

Prayer brings prophecy to fruition (Daniel 9). Gabriel told Daniel (Daniel 9:27) *At the beginning of your pleas for mercy a word went out.* Daniel's prayers were answered as soon as he began to pray. Gabriel informed Daniel that he was detained battling the Prince of Persia for twenty-one days before being able to confirm. Daniel obviously kept praying.

Sin and Forgiveness

Sin entered the world when fruit was taken from a tree. God placed the fruit back on a tree when Jesus was nailed to the cross

God cursed the ground to bear thorns for Adam. Jesus wore a crown of thorns to bear that curse in atonement for our sins.

God opened Adam's side to birth Eve. Jesus' side was pierced while on the cross to birth the Church. There would have been water and blood.

The first sin occurred in a garden. Jesus was buried in a garden.

Eve added to God's command by stating that she and Adam were not to touch the fruit on the tree. Jesus, the second Adam, reminded Mary Magdelene not to touch him. Jesus was *b resit, beginning*, the *firstfruit*.

Why was the stone rolled away from Jesus' tomb? Did he need the entrance opened so he could exit? The stone was rolled away so that we can enter in.

Paul's letters show a pattern of emphasizing that we were crucified with Christ and raised with him.

> *⁵ For if we have been united with him in a death like his, we shall certainly be united with him in a resurrection like his. – Romans 6:5 (ESV)*

> *3 ¹ If then you have been raised with Christ, seek the things that are above, where Christ is, seated at the right hand of God. ² Set your minds on things that are above, not on things that are on earth. ³ For you have died, and your life is hidden with Christ in God. – Colossians 3:1-3 (ESV)*

> *⁴ But God, being rich in mercy, because of the great love with which he loved us, ⁵ even when we were dead in our trespasses, made us alive together with Christ—by grace you have been saved— ⁶ and raised us up with him and seated us with him in the heavenly places in Christ Jesus, - Ephesians 2:4-6 (ESV)*

Lamentation

This may surprise many in today's world, but it is was actually common in the lives of ancient Israelites to the point of being expected.

It's easy for us to want to advise, counsel, and pray for those who weep when expressing their struggles with burdens. Sometimes, we just need to weep with those who weep, taking Romans 12:15 (ESV) seriously; ¹⁵ *Rejoice with those who rejoice, weep with those who weep.*

Waiting

Waiting. A dictionary defines it as *staying where one is or delaying action until a particular time or until something else happens*. It often connotes being dormant until an event occurs.

The Bible instructs us in several passages to wait upon the Lord. The Hebrew root word for *wait* is *qava* (kaw-vaw). Literally, it means *to bind together (perhaps by twisting); adhere to; cling to*. That seems to be a much more active meaning than depending on something to happen before we act.

What does God expect of us while waiting on Him? Many interpretations of Micah 6:8 suggest a focus on social justice; *act, to love*, and *walk* are verbs.

> *He has showed you, O man, what is good. And what does the LORD require of you? To act justly and to love mercy and to walk humbly with your God. – Micah 6:8*

Acting justly and loving mercy reflect God's character – God is just and merciful. Walking humbly with God requires maintaining a close relationship with God, binding to, adhering to, or clinging to Him.

What was God's purpose in creating man?

> *Male and female created he them; and blessed them, and called their name Adam, in the day when they were created. – Genesis 5:2 (KJV)*

The Hebrew word translated as *male* is *zakar*. While this word has both verb noun forms, God has told us that He is more interested in our heart and spirit than our physical attributes,

> *And he who searches our hearts knows the mind of the Spirit, because the Spirit intercedes for God's people in accordance with the will of God. – Romans 8:27 (NIV)*

Translating *zakar* in its verb tense (*zeker*) provides greater insight into God's purpose for mankind. The verb tense translation literally means *the remembering one*. What are we to remember if not God and his character? As in Micah 6:8, understanding and emulating God's character while walking humbly with Him is His purpose for us.

What is the first task God gave Adam? It was to emulate God in creation. How does God create? Genesis 1 tells us that God creates by speaking order into chaos and darkness. And Genesis 2:19 records God assigning Adam the task of speaking order into chaos by naming every creature.

> *[1] In the beginning God created the heaven and the earth. [2] And the earth was without form, and void; and darkness was upon the face of the deep. And the Spirit of God moved upon the face of the waters. [3] And God said, Let there be light: and there was light. – Genesis 1:1-3 (KJV)*

> *And out of the ground the Lord God formed every beast of the field, and every fowl of the air; and brought them unto Adam to see what he would call them: and whatsoever Adam called every living creature, that was the name thereof. – Genesis 2:19 KJV)*

Prayer is communication with God – listening and speaking. Prayer is a form of *walking humbly* with God as instructed in Micah 6:8.

Prayer is how we come to understand God's order, which includes knowing His character of justice and mercy. Binding to, adhering to, or clinging to Him in prayer allows us to grasp his character, enabling us to speak order into the chaos and darkness of our world, fulfilling our charge of dominion over the Earth.

What was the last command Jesus gave his disciples before ascending to heaven?

> *On one occasion, while he was eating with them, he gave them this command: "Do not leave Jerusalem, but wait for the gift my Father promised, which you have heard me speak about. Acts 1:4 (NIV)*

Jesus instructed them to wait. Did their waiting mean being dormant until the gift arrived?

> *They all joined together constantly in prayer, along with the women and Mary the mother of Jesus, and with his brothers. – Acts 1:14 (NIV)*

Their waiting was active, adhering and clinging to God through prayer.

The pattern is this: they prayed, the Holy Spirit came upon them, and they evangelized. Praying was breathing God in, and evangelism was exhaling what they had received. They spoke God's order into the chaos and darkness of this world.

Gratitude

Luke 17:11-19 recounts Jesus and his disciples traveling to Jerusalem, where they encountered ten men with leprosy. The men cried out to Jesus for healing. Jesus healed all of them and instructed them to show themselves to a priest as prescribed in the law of Moses.

After they were sanctified by the priest, one of them, a foreigner (not a Jew), returned to thank Jesus. This man was made whole, ἐκσῴζω (*eksōzō*).

All ten were healed of leprosy, but only one was made whole after expressing gratitude for the healing.

On the third day

The pattern of events *on the third day* appears throughout the Old and New Testaments, marking new beginnings and new life.

Creation

God separated the waters to reveal dry land calling it *Earth* on the third day. He created vegetation, plants that yielded seed, and fruit trees (Genesis 1:9-13).

Abraham's test

God told Abraham to sacrifice his only son Isaac. Abraham and Isaac set off for a place that God would show them. Genesis 22:4 tells us, *⁴ On the third day Abraham lifted up his eyes and saw the place from afar.*

Abraham considered Isaac raised from the dead. Hebrews 11:19 (ESV) confirms *¹⁹ He considered that God was able even to raise him from the dead, from which, figuratively speaking, he did receive him back.*

Ten Commandments

Once the Hebrews arrived at Mount Sinai during their exodus from Egypt, God told Moses, *For on the third day the Lord will come down on Mount Sinai in the sight of all the people.* – Exodus 19:11 (ESV)

Babylon

The return of God's people from captivity in Babylon is referred to as a resurrection (*on the third day*) in Hosea 6:1-2. (ESV)

> **6** *¹ "Come, let us return to the Lord; for he has torn us, that he may heal us; he has struck us down, and he will bind us up.*

> ² *After two days he will revive us; on the third day he*
> *will raise us up, that we may live before him.*

Jonah

Jonah was in the belly of a fish for three days before being restored. Jesus referenced Jonah as a sign that he would also give. Indeed, Jesus rose from death after three days in his tomb.

Water into wine

The first public miracle of Jesus occurred on the third day of a week when he turned water into wine at a wedding in Cana of Galilee. God's relationship with his people is often expressed as a marriage.

A Jewish wedding typically occurs in three parts, patterned after the third day of creation. This third day is doubly blessed, as God declared *it is good* twice. The first day, *shiddakhin*, involves the legal arrangements. The second day, *erusin* or *kiddushin*, is the betrothal, a period of sanctification. The third day, *rissuin*, is the day of marriage.

Jesus mother asked him to do something about the absence of wine for the wedding celebration. Jesus honored his mother by obeying her request. This honored the third of the Ten Commandments given at Mount Sinai. It is the first commandment that comes with an attached promise – long life and well-being.

Turning water into wine is reminiscent of Exodus 7:17-18 when God instructed Moses to strike the Nile with his staff, causing the water to turn to blood and resulting in the death of fish. Jesus turning water into wine demonstrated that he came to offer abundant life (John 10:10).

While the Tree of Knowledge of Good and Evil is usually depicted as an apple tree – an idea originating Song of Solomon 2:3 - Jewish thought has frequently associated the fruit with grapes and wine. Wine symbolizes eternal life, improving over time rather than decaying.

Why were there six pots?

Creation occurred in six days. The six pots of new wine symbolizes creation, and therefore serve as an announcement of Jesus' ministry to reconnect us with God's intention - his Plan A.

The stone pots were described as each containing 20 gallons. The pots themselves would have been heavy, and even heavier once filled with water. Yet the servants obeyed Jesus' instructions, likely wondering, *Why is he instructing us to provide water to the wedding guests instead of wine?* Yet they obeyed. The pattern of obedience, and the result from it, are also present in this passage.

To this day, a majority of Jewish weddings occur on Tuesdays, the third day of a week on the Hebrew calendar.

Accordance with Scriptures

When Paul wrote 1 Corinthians 15:4 (ESV), was he thinking only of Jonah, or was he also considering the pattern of events when he qualified his statement with *in accordance with the Scriptures*, given that *Scriptures* is plural?

> ⁴ *that he was buried, that he was raised on the third day in accordance with the Scriptures*

God's One-Offs

God is not limited to repeated patterns, and there may be patterns we are not readily aware of. Does he create uniqueness to prevent us from becoming complacent in our expectations and our faith regarding what he can and will do for us as his family?

All fruits have their seeds inside, except strawberries which have their seeds on the outside.

The lightning bug is the only cold source of light in nature.

Dimas was the criminal crucified at Jesus' right side (Gestas on the left).[35] He was not known for any good works, offerings, donations, sacrifices, or being baptized; he believed when belief was all he had left to give, and the pattern of that one act of believing was accepted.

Physical patterns

We are physical as well as spiritual beings.

Hunger and thirst are fundamental biological drives that motivate us to seek and consume food and water to maintain our health and well-being.

Children typically exhibit constant appetites for food and water, which are signs of physical growth that need to be fueled. A child's decreased hunger or increased thirst can be an early sign of illness, indicating that their physiological systems are trying to restore optimal health.

The Bible, from beginning to end, uses physical hunger and thirst as metaphors for maintaining spiritual health.

What we recognize as anxiety, fear, rejection, doubt, and emotional stress are emotional hungers and thirsts. These too need to be fed and watered, but in a spiritual sense. If these needs are met, they can manifest physically.

Wisdom, or discernment, is desirable in our lives. Wisdom is not a noun referring to any volume of knowledge; wisdom is a verb, representing the accurate application of God's will. How is the prophecy we find in Scripture, or in our life experiences, accurately applied?

---

[35] *The Gospel of Nicodemus* (formerly *The Acts of Pilate*), Chapter VII:3

PART IV
Application

Exile always precedes redemption. Exile can be imposed upon us, or we can effectively exile ourselves through the choices we make. God told Abraham that his descendants would dwell in a foreign land and be oppressed, but he also promised Abraham that they would emerge from that oppression with great wealth.

> *[13] Then the Lord said to Abram, "Know for certain that your offspring will be sojourners in a land that is not theirs and will be servants there, and they will be afflicted for four hundred years. [14] But I will bring judgment on the nation that they serve, and afterward they shall come out with great possessions. - Genesis 15:13-14 (ESV)*

After God delivered Israel from bondage in Egypt and brought them to Mt. Sinai, he had them rest there. They had endured oppression for 400 years; they were tired and battered. They needed to heal before they could continue their journey.

The pattern of work and rest allows us to renew, refresh, prosper, and revive. It is a time to reflect, remember, repurpose.

God used Moses to initiate nine miracles in Egypt to persuade Pharaoh to let the Hebrews go, with a tenth miracle occurring when the Red Sea was parted.

After approximately two years of resting at Mount Sinai, and engaging in several conversations with God on the mountain, God instructed Moses that it was time for the people to move on. Exodus 33:13 (ESV) records Moses saying to God, *[13] Now therefore, if I have found favor in your sight, please show me now your ways, that I may know you in order to find favor in your sight.* The English word *ways* is translated from the Hebrew word *derek*. Moses was asking for patterns of living a vibrant life.

> **2006** דֶּרֶךְ *(dĕ·rĕḵ): n,masc[36].; ≡ Str 1870; TWOT 453a—***1.** *LN 1.99–1.105* **way***, path, route, road, highway, i.e., a thoroughfare to physically get from one place to another (Ge 16:7), note: context will provide the size of the pathway, ranging from a narrow path to a major thoroughfare;* **2.** *LN 15.18– 15.26* **journey***, i.e., the act of moving from one place to another, with a destination, and usually planned route (Ge 24:27);* **3.** *LN 41.1–41.24* **conduct***, way of life, what is done, i.e., behave in a particular way, in the manner one conducts one's life, including habits, as a figurative extension of a thoroughfare (Pr 6:6; 25:4);* **4.** *LN 76* **strength***, vigor, might, i.e., power or force relatively greater than other entities (Pr 31:3; Hos 10:13), see also LN 74;* **5.** *LN 77 unit:* פָּנָה דֶּרֶךְ *(pā·nā(h) dĕ·rĕḵ) make ready, formally, turn the way, i.e., cause circumstances to be prepared for some event (Isa 40:3), note: for Isa 45:2 cj, see 2065; note: for niv text in Ps 119:37, see 1821[37]*

---

[36] masc. masculine

[37] Swanson, James. 1997. In *Dictionary of Biblical Languages with Semantic Domains : Hebrew (Old Testament)*, electronic ed. Oak Harbor: Logos Research Systems, Inc.

Now that we are enroute to our destination, there will be signs along the way indicating the need for rest or a change in the path or mode of transportation.

Watch for signs

Have you considered that Van Gogh's Starry Night is based on what he actually saw?

God speaks in many ways, his messages aren't always conveyed through verbal speech.

> **19** *To the choirmaster. A Psalm of David.*
> ¹ *The heavens declare the glory of God,*
> *and the sky above proclaims his handiwork.*
> ² *day to day pours out speech,*
> *and night to night reveals knowledge.*
> ³ *There is no speech, nor are there words,*
> *whose voice is not heard.*
> ⁴ *Their voice goes out through all the earth,*
> *and their words to the end of the world.*
> *In them he has set a tent for the sun,*
> ⁵ *which comes out like a bridegroom leaving his*
> *chamber,*
> *and, like a strong man, runs its course with joy.*
> ⁶ *Its rising is from the end of the heavens,*
> *and its circuit to the end of them, and there is nothing*
> *hidden from its heat. - Psalm 19:1-6 (ESV)*

Eyesight or Insight

There are two ways of seeing: eyesight and insight. The latter is more powerful than the former.

Around 300 BC, more than 1,800 years before Ferdinand Magellan's ships sailed around the globe, an astronomer named

Eratosthenes of Cyrene conceived and executed the first known accurate measurements of the earth's circumference without leaving the African continent.

Simple observation confirms that the world isn't flat. Through experiments with shadows cast by sunlit objects at long distances from one another, he understood that the sun's rays travel in parallel lines. He also knew that at each year's summer solstice the noon sun was directly overhead in the Egyptian city of Syene, shining at the bottom of a very deep well. At the same moment, the shadow cast by an obelisk in Alexandria (some 500 miles to the north) indicated that the sun was approximately 7.5 degrees from the zenith.

Eratosthenes measured the exact distance between the two cities. He gathered a group of people and trained them to take steps of fixed size by marching back and forth in a courtyard. He organized teams, assigned each a stretch of the 500 miles to pace off, and collected the total. In this way, he obtained a fairly accurate reading of the distance. (The word *mile* comes from the Latin word for *thousand*. A pace – or pair of steps – is about 5 feet long, and 1,000 paces gives us a mile.)

Eratosthenes knew that moving 1/48th of the circumference of a circle tilted the local vertical by an angle of 7.5 degrees, which matched the angle cast by the obelisk. Consequently, he concluded that the earth's circumference was 48 times the measured distance of 500 miles, equaling 24,000 miles. The modern measured value is 24,901 miles.

Behold. Beware.

We are witnessing a steady increase in chaos within our world and our communities. The primary instrument seems to be deception, leading us away from God.

When Elijah confronted the prophets of Baal, he asked the people, *How long with you go limping between two different opinions?* The English word *limping* in this verse (1 Kings 18:21) derives from the Hebrew פָּסַח (*pāsăḥ*), which also translates as *Passover.* This term would have resonated with the Israelites as a reference to God delivering them from bondage in Egypt.

Jesus warned us in Matthew 24, *See that no one leads you astray.* Isaiah 5:20 prophesied, *Woe to those who say that evil is good and good is evil, who put darkness for light and light for darkness.*

We are not here by accident. We are here for a moment like this.

As those moving in the prophetic, Paul instructed us we are to edify others. The Greek word translated as *edify* means *to build,* or *comfort,* understood here to be a promotion of growth in Christian character. I suggest we are in a time where we must build with a trowel in one hand and a sword in the other, as did those rebuilding Jerusalem after returning from Babylon.

We need not only to give encouraging words of *behold* to bless but also offer discerning words of *beware* to warn of danger. To beware means to be watchful. Prophets are types of watchmen who are expected to sound an alarm or warning when threats are evident.

Isaiah prophesied that the Messiah would be known as the Prince of Peace. The Hebrew title is *sar salom.*

שָׂרַר (*sā·răr*) means oversee a task with implied authority.

שָׁלוֹם (*šā·lôm*) means *peace, prosperity, i.e., an intact state of favorable circumstance.*

The noun *salom* is derived from the verbal root *salam,* which means *to restore,* in the sense of *replacing or providing what is needed in order to make someone or something whole and complete.* When we examine the meaning of the individual characters of *salom* שָׁלוֹם (Hebrew is read right to left) *shin-lamed-vav-mem*, it conveys **Destroy the authority that binds to chaos**. Obtaining and maintaining peace requires active spiritual warfare.

Until Jesus returns, peace is something we must contend for. It will require us to call on the authority of Jesus name. As stated earlier, authority is more significant than power because the righteous use of power stems solely from authority.

Hearing God's voice

When your friends call out to you upon spotting you in a store or at a park, do you associate their name with the sound of their voice and know who is calling your name before you turn to see them?

Hearing God's voice may begin simply, almost mundanely until you recognize it. It's akin to a scene from the 2010 movie of *The Karate Kid* featuring Jackie Chan and Jaden Smith.

Dre (Smith) arrives at Mr. Han's (Chan) house for his first lesson. Mr. Han leads Dre into an inner courtyard and has him stand in front of a pole with a wooden dowel protruding from it. *Take your jacket off. Hang it up. Take it down. Throw it on the ground. Pick it up. Put it on. Take it off….*and so it repeats.

This pattern is reminiscent of God first speaking to Samuel as a boy. Samuel initially thought, three successive times, that Eli had called him. After the third instance, Eli informed Samuel that it was God who was calling him.

Discernment

Discernment refers to the ability to distinguish fact from fallacy, one object from another. It involves testing incoming information by comparing it against standards we have accepted and believe.

What time is it?

God created time for the benefit of humanity rather than for himself. Here are some key reasons:

- To provide a framework for human existence and interaction. Time allows people to experience the world, live their lives, and engage with God meaningfully.
- To create a rhythm and purpose for human life. The structure of time consisting of seasons, days, and years offers a framework for work, rest, and spiritual practices.
- To offer opportunities for growth, change, and redemption. Time enables humans to learn, grow, and experience God's grace and salvation.
- To demonstrate God's faithfulness. The recurring cycles of nature and the consistent patterns of creation remind us of God's promises and unwavering nature.
- To establish a pattern of work and rest. The six-day creation story is often interpreted as a model for humans to follow, including a Sabbath day of rest.

The original Hebrew calendar began with the month of Tishri. When the Hebrews came out of Egypt, God instructed Moses to make the month of Nisan the first month to commemorate this deliverance and identified appointed times for them to celebrate, feast, remember that they were chosen and set apart.

The Hebrew calendar is based on lunar cycles. Typically, there are twelve months each year; however, an extra month is added every two to three years to keep the calendar aligned with the solar year and ensure Jewish holidays remain in their appropriate seasons. Specifically, an extra month, Adar II, is added seven times in a 19-year cycle because twelve lunar months comprise about 354 days, which is slightly shorter than the solar year.

Each month in the Hebrew calendar corresponds to a Hebrew letter, tribe, and number, all of which are believed to have prophetic significance.

Appointed time

The Hebrew term for appointed times, מוֹעֵד (*mô·ʿēḏ*), also known as the Jewish festivals or *moedim*, refers to seven specific days or periods in the Hebrew calendar designated as holy days. These appointed times, detailed in Leviticus 23 represent a set of celebrations with profound religious and historical significance for the Jewish people.

There was darkness before God created light, so the Hebraic day begins at 6:00 PM.

1. **Shabbat:** The weekly Sabbath, a day of rest and spiritual renewal, observed from sundown Friday to sundown Saturday.
2. **Pesach:** This holiday (Passover) commemorates the Israelites' liberation from slavery in Egypt and is celebrated for eight days.
3. **Feast of Unleavened Bread:** A part of Passover, celebrated for seven days, during which unleavened bread (matzah) is eaten to symbolize the haste of the Israelites' exodus from Egypt.

4. **Yom Habikkurim:** This festival occurs on the day after the Sabbath of the first day of Passover, commemorating the offering of the first fruits of the harvest.

5. **Shavuot:** Also known as Pentecost, this festival is celebrated fifty days after Passover and marks the giving of the Torah to Moses on Mount Sinai.

6. **Rosh Hashanah:** The Jewish New Year, celebrated on the first day of the month of Tishri, marking the beginning of the High Holy Days.

7. **Yom Kippur:** The holiest day of the Jewish year, a day of fasting and prayer dedicated to seeking forgiveness for sins.

8. **Sukkot:** Celebrated for eight days, this festival commemorates the Israelites' time in the desert after their exodus from Egypt and is marked by living in temporary shelters (sukkahs).

Appointed Feast [Heb. *môʿēḏ* (Lev. 23:2, 4, 37, 44; Nu. 10:10; 15:3; 29:39; etc.), *ḥaḡ* (Ezk. 45:17), *ʿaṣārâ* (Isa. 1:14)]; feast, solemn day, solemn feast, set feast, assembly; NEB appointed season, appointed festival, "sacred season appointed by the Lord" (Ezr. 3:5), sacred feast, place of assembly, etc.

When *môʿēḏ* means "appointed feast" it is usually in the plural (but cf. Lam. 2:6.; Hos. 12:9). When it is in the singular, a more normal rendering is "set time, season." Although *ḥaḡ* is translated "appointed feast" in Ezk. 45:17, its more usual meaning is "pilgrim feast" (the verbal form, *ḥaḡaḡ*, means to "make a pilgrimage"). The term *ʿaṣārâ* has the more usual meaning of "assembly," coming from a verb meaning to "hold in."

The festal times, exclusive of the sabbath, were kept three times a year. This threefold pattern of "appointed feasts" may reflect the agricultural environment of Canaan; they correspond to the times connected with planting, harvest, etc. The feast of the Passover is kept, along with the Feast of Unleavened Bread, for seven days, starting "in the first month, on the fourteenth day of the month" (Lev. 23:5). This means that the dates are Nisan 14–21. Framing the feast time are two convocations, one on the first day and one on the last. The ordinances for the keeping of the Passover and Feast of Unleavened Bread are found in Ex. 12:1–13:16; 23:15; 34:18ff; Lev. 23:5–14; Nu. 28:16–25; Dt. 16:1–8.

The Feast of Weeks was a one-day celebration, and although no precise date is given for it, the regulation states that it be fifty full days after the bringing of the barley offering at the Feast of Unleavened Bread (cf. Lev. 23:15f). This would put the Feast of Weeks in the early part of the third month. The basic texts ordaining this "appointed feast" are Lev. 23:15–21; Ex. 23:16; 34:22; Nu. 28:26–31; Dt. 16:9–12.

The Feast of Booths is ordained, among other places, in Lev. 23:33: "On the fifteenth day of this seventh month and for seven days is the feast of booths." This feast corresponds in time of year to the autumn ingathering of the crops. Earlier in the month (on the first day) the ram's horn is sounded, and on the tenth of the month the solemn fast (Heb. *ṣôm*) of *Yôm Kippur* ("day of atonement") occurs. For further details on the Feast of Booths see Ex. 23:16; 34:22; Lev. 23:33–36, 39–43; Nu. 29:12–32; Dt. 16:13–16.

There are several feasts celebrated in later Judaism which are not set out in the Torah. Two of these are *Ḥᵃnukkâ* ("dedication"), also known as the Festival of Lights, and *Pûrîm*. *Ḥᵃnukkâ* celebrates the cleansing of the temple of Judas Maccabeus in December, 164 b.c. (1 Macc. 4:52–59). It is observed starting on the twenty-fifth day of the ninth month. *Pûrîm* is a joyful celebration on the fourteenth day of the twelfth month, commemorating the

Jews' deliverance from Haman by Mordecai and Esther (Est. 9:23ff.)[38]

What does this inform us about the times we're currently in?

Remainder of current decade

God has never had a Plan B. He is graciously, and patiently reminding us of the identity he created for us. He is still restoring us as zakar and ezer.

Are there prophetic patterns in the Hebrew calendar? As of this writing (2025), we are in the Hebrew year 5785 - 5,785 years since creation.

The following is not meant to predict the future but to express opportunities from patterned insights in Scripture and the Hebrew calendar.

Decade of 5780

80 (Hebrew: pey; פ)

Pey also means *mouth*. We are in a decade of the mouth – when our speech, whether verbal or behavioral, determines our direction (the set of our sail) and what we create.

God instructed Moses to change the beginning of the Hebrew year to coincide with the Exodus when Israel came out of Egypt. This marks the Hebrew month of Nisan (in 2025, within April).

In the original Hebrew calendar, the month of Tishri is the beginning of the Hebrew year for years, sabbatical cycles, and jubilees. Although the functions of this new year primarily relate to the agricultural cycle and the beginning of a new harvest year, the Mishnah also begins to assign it conceptual and theological meaning.

---

[38] Ashley, T. R. 1979–1988. "Appointed Feast." In *The International Standard Bible Encyclopedia, Revised*, edited by Geoffrey W. Bromiley, 1:216. Wm. B. Eerdmans.

The Feast of Trumpets also begins on Tishri 1. Many scholars believe that Jesus was born on Tishri 1 based on John's description of constellations in Revelation 12. This date also marks the beginning of the reigns of all Davidic kings.

In this decade (5790), the number ninety (90) in Hebrew symbolizes righteousness.

This author believes there are five things God desires us to pursue in this decade. Initially, the five - unity, resilience, hope, faith, and love - seemed to be cyclical. However, it became clear that they do not form an endless circular pattern but rather an upward, outward, spiraling one.

Unity

Without unity, there is no community. We come together in community, where we support one another. Unity is one of the attributes God shared with us, as discussed by Tozer.

Diversity encourages us to focus on our differences, which separates us, and creates tension. Unity does not mean we are, or become, the same; it means we acknowledge our differences and come together in pursuit of a common goal, applying our differences as gifts to achieve that goal.

Consider the birds of the air and the fish of the sea. Though there are numerous individuals, the flock or school move as one. Nature itself proclaims God's design and intention for unity.

Breaking a horse for riding is not about conquering the horse or imposing your will on it. It's not about a rider and a horse. It's about the horse and rider becoming one.

We all seek three A's in life: Acceptance, Appreciation, and Approval. We give of ourselves when we receive (or perceive we receive) these A's from others or from a group. These A's can be why some individuals join street gangs, as they find these A's there.

The three A's can lead to either blessing or curse.

The Hebrew word translated into forms of the English *bless* is *baruch*. *baruch* means *to bow*, or *take a knee*. Either of those actions is a recognition of value. Blessing someone is recognition of their value as a child, an imager, of God.

Unity is fundamentally about relationships with others. Addiction, whether through substance or activities, is less about the substance or activity itself and more about the connection or relationship with others.[39] The choices we make in this regard are influenced by dopamine, a substance released in our brains in response to either pain or pleasure.[40]

Resilience

Support within a community fosters resilience – both individually and collectively.

Resilience is often viewed as the ability to return to a previous state after experiencing stress. While this may describe a desirable outcome for inanimate objects it does not apply to humans, who can become stronger and more capable through challenges. We must ask ourselves whether we truly want to return to our former state.

For us, resilience signifies our ability to overcome life's trials. Even physical growth from early childhood to adulthood can be physically painful. Unity and support from others mean we do not have to face these challenges alone.

Overcoming does not imply a lack of fear; it means we confront and manage our fears. We have all faced challenges that likely evoke varying degrees of fear. The Bible contains numerous stories of overcoming fear.

---

[39] Alexander, B. K. (1987). The disease and adaptive models of addiction: A framework evaluation. Journal of Drug Issues 17, pp. 47-66.

[40] Lembke, A. (2021). *Dopamine Nation: Finding balance in the age of indulgence*. Dutton.

Courage doesn't mean you're not afraid. It means you saddle up and ride anyway. – John Wayne

The remarkable thing about God is that when you fear God, you fear nothing else, whereas if you do not fear God, you fear everything else. – Oswald Chambers

Becoming more resilient assures us that we can hope for something greater.

If you are going to be used by God, He will take you through a number of experiences that are not meant for you personally at all. They are designed to make you useful in His hands, and to enable you to understand what takes place in the lives of others.[41]

At age five, I developed cold sores on the lower lid of my right eye. If you've experienced cold sores, you know they cause significant itching and are caused by a form of the herpes virus. At that age, when something itches, the instinct is to rub or scratch it. In my case, the rubbing caused the sores to break, transferring the virus to my right eye and resulting in a herpetic ulcer.

The ulcer caused intense pain and extreme sensitivity to light. My parents consulted with numerous doctors, all of whom informed them that my right eye would need to be removed, or I could lose both eyes. My parents persisted in seeking referrals to doctors who might save my right eye.

I have vague memories of the trip to a children's hospital in Dayton, Ohio for one of these referrals and can still envision the large ward filled with children facing various medical needs.

The doctor at the children's hospital cauterized the ulcer on my right eye with the tip of a toothpick, drew blood from my

---

[41] Oswald Chambers, & Reimann, J. (2018). *My Utmost for His Highest*. November 5. Discovery House.

arm, and prescribed placing two drops of my blood into my right eye twice daily.

The prescribed treatment (pattern) was meant to nourish the healthy cells to the extent that the unhealthy virus could not progress and would eventually be inactivated. I have come to realize that this is a pattern that applies to spiritual healing as well as physical healing – nourish what is healthy so the unhealthy cannot thrive.

I also learned that pain is not a problem; it is a messenger indicating that something is out of order. Instead of focusing on, and addressing, the pain, determine what is out of order, and restore order.

My parents demonstrated God's hesed love toward me; love that is fully committed, unwavering, and motivated by hope. This, more than anything else I've experienced in my life, has taught me resilience that leads to hope.

Hope

Hope is the expectation or belief in the fulfillment of something desired. Present hurts and uncertainties about the future create a constant need for hope.

> *The patriarch Abraham exemplifies faith and hope. In spite of the realities he faced, no distrust made him waver concerning the promise of God, but he grew strong in his faith as he gave glory to God (Romans 4:20, 21).*

Christian faith and hope, like Abraham's, are grounded in the faithfulness of God. As the apostle Paul expressed during his struggles, *Why, we felt that we had received the sentence of death; but that was to make us rely not on ourselves but on God who raises the dead; he delivered us from so deadly a peril, and he will deliver us; on him we have set our hope and he will deliver us again* (2 Corinthians 1:9, 10). Thus, hope is not irrational; it is based upon God, who has proven himself faithful. Biblical hope is hope rooted in the expectation of God will do in the future.[42]

Faith

Hope held becomes faith. Faith is the evidence of what is not visible.

Faith is a state of unwavering trust in God. It is central to Christianity, and its significance for today's believer is underscored by the fact that Protestantism emerged through the rediscovery of the powerful declaration, *The just shall live by faith* (Romans 1:17 KJV).

Faith in both the Old and New Testaments encompasses several meanings. It may denote simple trust in God or in the Word of God, and at other times it may equate to active obedience. It can also find expression in affirming creedal statements, thus the entire body of received Christian teaching or truth. In Colossians 2:7, the term suggests something to be accepted as a whole and embodied in personal life. In 2 Timothy 4:7 Paul testifies to having *kept the faith.*[43]

> **11** *¹ Now faith is the assurance of things hoped for, the conviction of things not seen. ² For by it the people of old received their commendation. ³ By faith we understand that the universe was created by the word of God, so that what is seen was not made out of things that are visible. – Hebrews 11:1-3 (KJV)*

[42] McAlister, Paul K. 1988. "Hope." In *Baker Encyclopedia of the Bible*, 1:997. Grand Rapids, MI: Baker Book House.
[43] Lyon, Robert W. 1988. "Faith." In *Baker Encyclopedia of the Bible*, 1:761. Grand Rapids, MI: Baker Book House.

Faith is not a feeling. Faith is where we find protection under God's wing - next to his heart.[44]

There are stages in life when there is no storm, no crisis, when we do our human best; it is when a crisis arises that we instantly reveal upon whom we rely. If we have been learning to worship God and to trust Him, the crisis will reveal that we will go to the breaking point and not break in our confidence in Him.[45]

God puts no limits on faith, and faith puts no limits on God.

Love

Love is not merely a feeling or an emotion; it is an integral part of who we are. The more we allow someone to become part of who we are, the deeper the love. That can, and will, get messy.

Nevertheless, love deals frankly with human weakness and wickedness. Jesus prays for Peter, but not that he shall be spared temptation; he rebukes disciples, warns Jerusalem and Judas, makes Peter painfully retract his denials, accepts that love may have to lay down its life. Christ's love is no timid meekness, no sentimental mildness, inoffensive and ineffectual, helpless in face of the world's evil. It is a strong determination to seek others' highest good in all circumstances, at any cost. On that simple but demanding principle hang all moral obligation and divine law. To love is enough.[46]

Intimacy and community come from love, not the other way around. So instead of pursuing intimacy, we should pursue love. Only then do we discover intimacy. That is what Ruth is doing. Ruth's living death for Naomi has created a powerful

[44] Miller, P. E. (2014). *A Loving Life*. Crossway.
[45] Oswald Chambers, & Reimann, J. (2018). *My Utmost for His Highest*. April 12. Discovery House.
[46] White, R.E.O. 1988. "Love." In *Baker Encyclopedia of the Bible*, 2:1357–58. Grand Rapids, MI: Baker Book House.

community between the two of them. John describes this pattern in Jesus's death: He *would die for the nation … to gather into one the children of God* (John 11:51–52). A dying love creates the possibility of oneness.[47]

Without love, there is no unity.

The following is an excerpt from the final chapter of *A Loving Life* by Paul E. Miller, one of the most powerful books I have ever read. In describing love, I cannot express it any better. Miller quotes from B.B Warfield, revealing the depth of Warfield's understanding of love:

Everything Ruth does—from walking through the gates ignored and unthanked to giving her newborn son to Naomi—is a function of her love for Naomi. She risks her honor by lying at the feet of Boaz, alone and vulnerable, in order to restore Naomi's family line. By marrying an older man she almost assures herself that she will again be a widow. This complete absence of self reflects the mind of Christ. B. B. Warfield wrote this about Christ's self-giving:

> *He did not cultivate self, even His divine self: He took no account of self. He was not led … into the recesses of His own soul to brood morbidly over His own needs . … He was led by His love for others into the world, to forget Himself in the needs of others, to sacrifice self once for all upon the altar of sympathy. Self-sacrifice brought Christ into the world. And self-sacrifice will lead us, His followers, not away from, but into the midst of men. Wherever men suffer, there will we be to comfort. Wherever men strive, there will we be to help. Wherever men fail, there will we be to uplift. Wherever men succeed, there will we*

---

[47] Miller, P. E. (2014). *A Loving Life*. Crossway.

be to rejoice. Self-sacrifice means not indifference to our times and our fellows: it means absorption in them. It means forgetfulness of self in others. It means entering into every man's hopes and fears, longings and despairs: it means manysidedness of spirit, multiform activity, multiplicity of sympathies. It means richness of development. It means not that we should live one life, but a thousand lives—binding ourselves to a thousand souls by the filaments of so loving a sympathy that their lives become ours.[48]

Warfield's vision of living "a thousand lives—binding ourselves to a thousand souls by the filaments of so loving a sympathy that their lives become ours" is a perfect description of the Christian life. Every need, every person, is an opportunity to live another life. It is wonderful to connect with friends, but by itself it can feed tribalism, where your identity comes from your group. We've seen repeatedly how the quest for a feeling of love leads to a fractured self, manipulating or posturing. As our culture lurches back to pagan tribalism, recreating the American high school on a broader scale, we must ask the Jesus questions, "Who's lonely? Who doesn't fit in? Whom can I love?" Instead of trying to join a community, we can create community. We really have only two choices in life: a divided self or a multiplied self. We can either splinter into a thousand selves or live a thousand lives.

I wondered why Warfield understood so much about love until I discovered that on his honeymoon, while waiting on a train platform, his wife was struck by lightning. She became an invalid for the rest of her life. Warfield learned how to love in the trenches. When I mentioned this to a friend, he said, "What's

---

[48] Benjamin B. Warfield, *The Person and Work of Christ* (Philadelphia: Presbyterian and Reformed, 1950), 574.

the point of living if that happens to your wife?" I said, "Don't worry. The further you get into love, the easier it becomes.'"[49]

Through end of the decade

The following outlines a perceived pattern of potential based on the Hebrew calendar. This potential exists because we, like those who came before, have an the opportunity to speak order into the world we live in.

Decade of 5780
Gregorian calendar: 9/29/2019 thru 9/27/2030

80 (Hebrew: *pey*, פ)

Pey also means *mouth* or *speech*. We are in a decade of the mouth – when our speech, whether verbal or behavioral, determines our direction (the set of our sail), and shapes what we create.

Hebrew year: 5785
Gregorian calendar: 10/2/2024 thru 9/22/2025
10/2/2024 Tishri 1, Rosh Hashanah, Feast of Trumpets

Hey (5; ה) – breath, air, known identity, formed from dalet + gimmel, representing the unification of giving (gimmel) and receiving (dalet)

Holy Spirit, wind, thought, action, word, behold, power, grace, unity, maturity, alertness, service, awakening, anointing, prayer, being filled, being prepared

Without love there is no unity

> *The anointing oil recipe given by God has five ingredients (Exodus 30:22-25)*

[49] Miller, P. E. (2014). *A Loving Life*. Crossway.

This is a year of Jubilee. Captives set free. Debt forgiven. Property returned. The land and the people are to rest.

This a year to anoint the kings and priests as new identity. Kingly authority mindset. Priestly authority to understand spiritual warfare. Contend for the altars – destroy altars to false gods, and rebuild altar to Yahweh.

The year 5785 is a year of power, maturity and unity. This is based on the number five at the end of this figure of 5785. It begins with 5 (breath of God), and ends with 5 (breath of God).

The fifth Hebrew letter, *hey*, has a numerical value of five. Its pictographic meaning encompasses breath, air, spirit, femininity, and behold (to make known). As a prefix, it serves as the definite article "the", indicating something whose identity is known.

On the fifth day of creation, the birds and fish were created. They move quickly and carry seed throughout the earth in their migrations, demonstrating unity. Like them, we are anointed and filled with the Spirit to carry God's Seed, the Gospel, throughout the earth. Observe how perfectly synchronized the movements of creation were on day five (Genesis 1:21), flocks of birds and schools of fish in the *mayim* (waters) and *shamayim* (heavens). Though they are numerous, they flow as one fluid body.

This is a time of wind and water; either or both will test foundations.

Foundations are the solid base upon which a secure structure can be built; they are chiefly for the base of the temple. This term is often figuratively applied to Jesus Christ and the apostles and prophets as the secure foundation of the Church. Obedience to the teachings of Jesus Christ is the true foundation of Christian living.

This year, focus on returning males to *zeker* (*the remembering one*) and females to *ezer (strength, formally, help, i.e., power to accomplish a task*) roles and offices.

Hebrew year: 5786
Gregorian calendar: 9/23/2025 thru 9/11/2026
9/23/2025 Tishri 1, Rosh Hashanah, Feast of Trumpets

vav (6; ו) – spike, hook, connector, conjunction, man, mankind

Continuation, connecting what is and what is to come, transitioning from 5785 into 5787

The word *vav* actually means "hook." A hook holds two things together and serves to connect the spiritual and physical realms.

Hebrew number six signifies fulfillment. Man was created on the sixth day.

Given the reference to man, this year will initiate a shaking, prompting individuals to decide whether they are connected to God. This shaking will strengthen the Church as many believers will return and reconnect to their first love. The connection also refers to the convergence of the spiritual and physical.

Shaking is a process that can blend (make homogeneous) or separate.

Hebrew year: 5787
Gregorian year: 9/12/2026 thru 10/1/2027
9/12/2026 Tishri 1, Rosh Hashanah, Feast of Trumpets

zayin (7; ז) – crown, weapon, sword, sustain

Many letters of the alef-beis bear crowns, called *zayenin*. The word *zayin* also means *weapons* - as in the phrase *k'lei zayin* (the *zayin* looks like a sword). Additionally, *zayin* means *zun, to sustain*. These three definitions are interrelated. Shabbos (Sabbath), the crown of Creation, blesses and sustains the following week. By observing Shabbos, one accesses these blessings, which provides the weapon to overcome negativity, especially the *yetzer hara*, the *evil inclination*.

Shabbat (Hebrew: שַׁבָּת, also known as "Shabbos" or the "Sabbath") is the Jewish day of rest and celebration beginning on Friday before sunset ending the following evening after nightfall. Shabbat is central to Jewish life.

The mouth can be a weapon. Know when and how to use it, and when and how not to.

Hebrew year: 5788
Gregorian calendar: 10/2/2027 thru 9/20/2028
10/2/2027 Tishri 1, Rosh Hashanah, Feast of Trumpets

Chet (8; ח) (also spelled Ches and Het). The meaning of the word *ches* is *chayos*, which translates to *life*.

Life can only be considered true when infused with Godliness, for the body alone is temporary, and anything temporary cannot be true.

The eighth letter of the *aleph-beis* is *chet*. According to the Arizal, the *chet* fuses two letters: the *vav* and the *zayin*. On top of the *vav* and *zayin* is a *chatoteret,* (literally a *hump*) — a bridge that unites the two. In essence, *vav* represents the male principle (the husband). While *zayin* represents the female principle (the wife). God serves as the bridge linking them. The Maggid of Mezritch illuminates the verse *The woman of valor is the crown of her husband* to show that *zayin*, the crown, signifies the role of the woman of valor in safeguarding the man.

The design of the *chet* represents another type of bridge. If the relationship between *vav* (man) and *zayin* (woman) is to be complete, the two are united beneath a *chuppah* (marriage canopy). The form of the *chet* resembles a marriage canopy. The word *chuppah*, חופה, even begins with a *chet*, as *chuppah* means *chet po* - *chet* (God, man, and woman) is *po* (*here*). *Chet* represents the heart of marriage. Man and woman are truly united only when they stand together beneath the *chuppah* with the third partner, God.

Hebrew year: 5789
Gregorian calendar: 9/21/2028 thru 9/9/2029
9/21/2028 Tishri 1, Rosh Hashanah, Feast of Trumpets

tet (9; ט) – good or best

The design of the *tet* resembles a pot or vessel with an inverted rim, symbolizing hidden or inverted goodness. Another interpretation of the *tet* is that it represents a person bending their head to God in prayer and thanks. How are these two concepts connected? As explained previously, the letter *chet* represents the concept of marriage. After the union between husband and wife, and God willing, conception follows. The *tet* represents the hidden good that resides within the womb (the vessel) of the mother. This hidden good is actualized through a person's prayers to God, asking Him for a healthy child.

The numeric value of *tet* is nine. This corresponds to the nine months of pregnancy. Furthermore, the number nine is a "true" number. Truth or אמת (*emet*), is spelled with *aleph* (the first letter) of the aleph-beis; *mem* (the middle letter); and the *tav* (the last letter). The lesson is that something true must be true throughout its beginning, middle, and end.

Hebrew year: 5790 (technically, this is the last year of the decade)
Gregorian calendar: 9/10/2029 thru 9/27/2030
9/10/2029 Tishri 1, Rosh Hashanah, Feast of Trumpets

Tzadik (90, צ) 1. Righteous 2. Hunt
The Hebrew word צֶדֶק (*ṣĕ·ḏĕq*) (righteousness):

> **7406** צֶדֶק (*ṣĕ·ḏĕq*): n.masc.; ≡ Str 6664; TWOT 1879a—
> **1.** LN 88.12–88.23 **righteousness**, *justice, rightness,*

*i.e., the act of doing what is required according to a standard (Ps 7:9[EB 8]); **2**. LN 88.39–88.45 **honesty**, fairness, accuracy, i.e., an act of which is proper according to a standard, and not deviant in any way (Lev 19:36); **3**. LN 12.1–12.42 **Righteousness**, i.e., a title of the LORD (Jer 23:6; 33:16); **4**. LN 56.20–56.34 **justice**, i.e., the act of fairly deciding what is right in a legal case, without prejudice (Dt 16:20), note: further study may yield more domains*[50]

Malki Tzedek (*Melchizedek*) was a royal priest, a king and a priest, known as a **righteous** king. Jesus is referred to as being in the line of *Melchizedek*. The decade of 5780's focuses on God's word being spoken (pey) throughout the earth to bring righteousness.

Freedom and peace are not free.

Isaiah 9:6 prophesied of Jesus, referring to him as the Prince of Peace.

The Hebrew is *sar salom* (shalom). סָרַר (*sā·răr*) means *to oversee a task with implied authority.*

שָׁלוֹם (*šā·lôm*) does mean *peace*, prosperity, i.e., an intact state of favorable circumstance.

Each Hebrew letter can represent objects in life (mouth, door, hand, shepherd, etc.) and thus indicate context. The life objects each letter in a word represents can comprise a phrase that provides context.

The noun *salom* is derived from the verbal root *salam*, which means *to restore*, in the sense of providing what is needed to make someone or something whole and complete. It is usually translated into English as *peace* If we examine the meaning of the individual letters שָׁלוֹם (Hebrew is read right to left)

---

[50] James Swanson, *Dictionary of Biblical Languages with Semantic Domains : Hebrew (Old Testament)* (Oak Harbor: Logos Research Systems, Inc., 1997).

shin-lamed-vav-mem, it reads **Destroy the authority that binds to chaos**. This is spiritual warfare.

Peace is not free; it requires struggle to defeat chaos in our lives to attain and maintain it.

Until Jesus returns, peace is something we must contend for, requiring us to call on the authority of Jesus name. Authority is determined by the proximity to the author.

Revival

We can't revive that which was not previously alive. –
Leonard Ravenhill

Revival is not about new converts to the Christian faith; it is about awakening those who already profess belief in Jesus as the Christ.

There are patterns in revival throughout the Bible.

Abram the Hebrew

In Hebrew, *abra* can have multiple meanings. It can mean *father of many*, *father of a multitude*, or be a diminutive form of Abraham or Abram. It can also mean *I will create* or be part of the phrase *I will create as I speak*. Additionally, in a biblical context, *abra* can be a title for Sarah, the wife of Abraham, recognizing her role in giving birth to the Hebrew nation.[51]

After separating the people at Babel, effectively disinheriting them, God called Abram and Sarai out of Ur as a means of revival for mankind. It was God's plan to remind them where their believing loyalty belonged.

---

[51] Ancestry.com, https://www.ancestry.com/first-name-meaning/abra

Passover

While the ten plagues God sent upon Egypt were spiritual warfare against the gods of Egypt to demonstrate that their gods were not all powerful, God's deliverance of the descendants of Jacob from Egypt was a revival for those descendants.

The Hebrews had been captive in Egypt for 400 years. They likely were focused on their plight rather than on God. Their witnessing of God overpowering the Egyptian gods revealed to the Hebrews who Yahweh is.

The Nile turns to blood. The Nile was considered the source of life in Egypt, providing water and food. Two Egyptian gods were associated with the Nile: Hapi, their god of the Nile who provided fish, birds, and fertile soil (deposited in fields when the Nile flooded), and Khnum, the potter god, believed to form humans on a potter's wheel from the silt of the Nile.

Yahweh turning the Nile to blood, killing the living things in it, showed that Hapi and Knum were not all powerful.

Frogs. It was not unusual for frogs to come onto land from the Nile during floods. They were seen as a sign of fertility and new life for the land and the people. The Egyptian goddess Heket associated with childbirth, creation, and grain germination, and thought to be the wife of Khnum.

The midwives choosing to fear Yahweh rather than obey Pharoah demonstrated that Heket could not favor the Egyptians over the Hebrews.

Stinging gnats. Moses had Aaron strike the earth, causing dust to rise and become stinging gnats. This was a direct confrontation with the Egyptian god Geb, whom the Egyptians believed was the god of the earth. Instead of the earth producing food, it brought forth stinging gnats causing painful sores.

Geb was believed to have the power to hold the dead in their graves or release them to the afterlife. If Geb couldn't control something as small as a gnat, how could he control death?

Flies. Khepri, one of the Egyptian gods perceived to be among the most powerful, was even believed to control insects and was thought to move the sun across the sky each day.

This plague revealed Khepri's ineptitude at controlling insects.

Livestock. Hathor was the Egyptian goddess of love, fertility, women, and cleansing the land of unbelievers.

This plague insulted to the religious hierarchy, affecting calves, cows, and bulls that were all worshipped by the Egyptians.

Boils. Ancient Egypt had numerous gods and goddesses thought to bring healing or infirmity.

They performed rituals for healing, including a particularly gruesome one that involved offering a human sacrifice, burning the victim alive on an altar, and then scattering the ashes into the air, believing this would bring healing to their people.

When Moses tossed a handful of soot into the air that brought boils on Egyptians, it directly confronted the Egyptian ritual, and demonstrated the powerlessness of their gods.

Hail. The Egyptian goddess Nut was associated with sky, separating the forces of chaos from the ordered cosmos. She was the wife of Geb, the earth god, and particularly linked to the night sky.

When God sent hail, it showed that Nut was powerless to protect the Egyptians from chaos from the sky.

Locusts. Shu was the god of wind, Hephri was the goddess who guarded the grain, Renenutet was the goddess who guarded the harvest, Geb was the god of the earth, and Heset was the god of plenty.

God sent locusts on the east wind, devoured the grain, wiped out the harvest, stripped the earth of all vegetation, and removed the Egyptians' prosperity.

Darkness. Exodus 10:21 tells us that the darkness could even be "felt." Verse 10:22 describes it as thick, a total absence of light.

The highest god in Egypt was Ra, the sun god, the bringer of light. His counterpart was the god Apep, who ruled darkness.

By sending a prolonged total darkness, Yahweh demonstrated power over Ra. Meanwhile, with sunlight in Goshen, where the Hebrews lived, Yahweh showed authority over Apep.

Death of the firstborn. One of the highest gods of Egypt was Pharaoh himself. Yahweh provided a path to escape the final plague. However, since Pharaoh would not yield, the final plague would take what was most important to him - his first-born son, who was next in line to be Pharaoh.

Once the Hebrews reached Sinai, they remained there for two years. After 400 years of slavery, they were battered and in need of healing and strengthening, and more importantly, to get to know God.

Afikomen. The portion of matzah eaten near the end of the Passover seder (meal) commemorates the occasion when the feast culminated with eating the paschal lamb that had been sacrificed in the Temple.[52] Each Jewish household places three matzah on the seder table. One of the matzah is broken into two pieces, and one of those pieces is wrapped and hidden in the house for three days. The children of the household are sent through the house to find it, and then include it in a final celebration and remembrance.

---

[52] Geaves, Ron. 2002. "Afikomen." In *Continuum Glossary of Religious Terms*, 8–9. London; New York: Continuum.

Pentecost

Pentecost is a Christian observance that commemorates the day the Holy Spirit came upon Jesus' disciples while they were gathered in prayer and worship in what is referred to as *the upper room*. This event occurred 50 days after Jesus' resurrection.

The Hebrew word Shavuot means *weeks*. It refers to the day after the Festival of Weeks. which God prescribed for them to celebrate the harvest by giving of the first fruits of their harvest as a sacrificial offering to him. Shavuot is celebrated the day after seven weeks (49 days) following Passover, with the offering given on the 50th day. Pentecost and Shavuot occur on the same day.

Torah, which contains instructions, directions, and patterns was given at Sinai on Shavuot. It was a supernatural event, both individually and corporately. Fire was present on the mountain. Shavuot is one of the three appointed pilgrimage feasts.

The Holy Spirt came upon the disciples as fire, providing instructions, directions, and patterns on Pentecost. Jews had gathered in Jerusalem from many nations for Shavuot, marking it as a supernatural event, both individually and corporately.

Fire changes things. It purges, purifies, and prepares vessels for new provision.

Every revival since God called Abram and Sarai out of Ur has begun and continued through prayer and worship. The record of Herrenhut is a prime example.

Herrenhut

Have you heard of Herrenhut, Germany? One of the most impactful revivals in history began there, following a pattern of prayer and worship.

In 1727, a group of Moravians fleeing persecution in Czechoslovakia, immigrated to Germany. They were allowed to settle on the estate of Count Nicholas Zinzindorf, and the village they built was named Herrenhut, meaning *the Lord's watch*.

On August 13, 1727, they went to the nearby village of Bertlesdorf to participate in communion service. Partway through an address by Count Zinzindorf, the Holy Spirit fell upon the congregation. They described it as *the fire of God fell*.

After this experience, they acknowledged that God was with them and wondered how they could continue in His presence. They turned to the Bible and found God's instructions to keep fire burning on the alter in Leviticus 6:12-13. They determined to keep *the fire on the altar* by dividing the day into watches and took turns praying 24 hours a day, 7 days a week. They continued this practice for about 120 years! Now that's following a pattern!

As a result, the glory of God rested in their midst.

The Spirit of God began to send them out as missionaries. They traveled all over the world. In the early 1700's, there were missionaries from Herrenhut in Greenland, England, North America, South America, South Africa, among Australian aborigines, and even in Tibet. One of the individuals saved in England due to these missionaries was John Wesley. At that time, England was in a dreadful situation – similar to France before its revolution. Wesley traveled to Herrenhut, caught the revival, and carried it back to England. Secular historians likely acknowledge that the revival Wesley brought to England saved it from bloody revolution.

The revival that began in Herrenhut spread through England and crossed the Atlantic. In America, it was called the Great Awakening. As it swept through the colonies, church attendance in America doubled. Benjamin Franklin[53] described it this way this way: *From being thoughtless and indifferent about religion,*

---

[53] *The Electric Ben Franklin*, page 49, https://www.ushistory.org/franklin/autobiography/page49.htm#google_vignette

it seemed as if all the world was growing religious. One could not walk through a town in an evening without hearing psalms being sung in different families on every street.

The US Constitution was written, for the most part, by men whose lives had been touched by this awakening. America is the country it is today because, back in a tiny corner of eastern Germany, there was continual praise and prayer.

Epilogue/Conclusion

Patterns are models that can be applied and followed. They exist and are available through God's creation, which includes ourselves. They are ever-present in us and around us, part of who we are. They provide for and care for us. They are best realized when we use them in unity with one another.

As imagers of God, we are able to imagine. This requires developing our creativity.

Individuals known for their creativity have methods to activate it.

After World War II, a group of international representatives, led by Michael Mihalko, studied how creative individuals activated their creativity. Mihalko wrote a book entitled *Thinkertoys* which describes some of the techniques used by creative people.[54]

Some of the advised techniques for changing daily habits include:

- Take a different route to work
- Change your sleeping hours
- Change your working hours
- Change your break habits
- If you normally read nonfiction, read fiction
- If you usually drink coffee, drink juice

---

[54] Michalko, M. (2007). *Thinkertoys*. The Rocks Campus Ten Speed Press.

- Change the type of restaurants you go to
- Take a bath instead of a shower
- Listen to a different radio station each day

Einstein used to take naps to find breakthroughs when he struggled with solving problems. Edison went fishing, without any bait on the end of his line, so fish wouldn't disturb his thinking.

These same principles can be applied to activating prophetic vision, observation and understanding. In other words, you will begin to see or recognize patterns in life that you may have previously missed. For example, consider the following....

Do you see the word FLOP in the image just below? Do you see anything else?

Is the image below just a collection of random black shapes?

Even to your old age

My family moved from Illinois to Indiana at the end of August 2017. My wife had employment in our new location before we moved, but I did not.

Every weekday morning, after taking our children to school, I would return home to read from the Bible and pray, followed by some job hunting.

Isaiah had long been a go-to book for me. I had read through it, and studied it. Yet on this day, October 13, 2017, the text of Isaiah 46:4 (NIV) seemed to jump off the page in bold letters:

> *⁴ Even to your old age and gray hairs I am he, I am*
> *he who will sustain you.*
> *I have made you and I will carry you; I will sustain*
> *you and I will rescue you.*

I wasn't sure why, but I perceived God was highlighting it. I decided to read that verse daily. It fit with the lesson I learned about God's hesed love at age five.

I found employment and began the job at the beginning of November.

Not long after, I began feeling lethargic. My wife noticed I looked pale and suggested I go to the ER. After an examination, and several tests, I was informed that all of my organs were sounding alarms, but a definite diagnosis wasn't clear. I spent a couple of days in a hospital room for further testing until a nephrologist came in to inform me that my kidneys were inflamed and not functioning.

As my family left the hospital that evening, one of my sons came alongside of my bed and asked if I was going to die. I assured him I wasn't, and recited Isaiah 46:4 as my confirmation.

After several months of dialysis, my kidney function returned.

The times we live in

A meta-analysis of prophecies over the last 15 years reveals a common theme that can be expressed in a single word *shaking*. This is not a future event but one that has already begun. John Paul Jackson's revelation, which he called *The Perfect Storm*, may be the most comprehensive. Shaking is a process that can both blend and separate. This pattern is echoed in Haggai, which encourages the rebuilding of the Temple….

> *Work, for I am with you, declares the Lord of hosts,*
> *⁵ according to the covenant that I made with you*
> *when you came out of Egypt. My Spirit remains in*
> *your midst. Fear not. ⁶ For thus says the Lord of*
> *hosts: Yet once more, in a little while, I will shake*
> *the heavens and the earth and the sea and the dry*
> *land. – Haggai 2:4-6 (ESV)*

This theme appears again in Hebrews:

> *²⁶ At that time his voice shook the earth, but now*
> *he has promised, "Yet once more I will shake not*
> *only the earth but also the heavens." ²⁷ This phrase,*
> *"Yet once more," indicates the removal of things that*
> *are shaken—that is, things that have been made—*
> *in order that the things that cannot be shaken may*
> *remain. – Hebrews 12:26-27 (ESV)*

The Information Age

AI (Artificial Intelligence) has become a hot topic, and buzzword in our current day. While AI does offer a great deal of digital functionality that results in increased productivity, there is nothing artificial about AI. It is simply a clever marketing scheme. Much like prophecy – behold and/or beware - AI is about binary choice. After all, computers are designed to mimic the human brain to aid mankind in thought processes – and increase our productivity.

A computer or computer system can do only four things:

- store data,
- move data,
- compare data,
- and add (all mathematical functions are executed through binary addition)

A computer consists of a group of electric circuits, where each circuit is either open or closed, on or off, one or zero, true or false, yes or no. AI results from technological advancements (real intelligence) coming to a point where chip makers and developers have learned to dynamically combine circuits (small segments of binary logic) that assess data input, leading to the highest statistical potential response. While it does assist in reaching conclusions, it is not intelligent. Disconnect the electrical source of power, and it becomes essentially worthless.

A challenging question arises: *What is AI doing with my data?* Don't be deceived. Those who market AI are learning about you from the data you provide as input into the decision-making process of AI.

God has presented us with patterns of binary choice. We each decide whether to choose humility that honors God's provision and blessing or pride in living life our own way. This choice is often expressed in the Bible as the struggle between good and evil. The Bible even prophesies that what is good will be called evil, and what is evil will be called good.

Prophecy serves as an act of reminding our fellow man where our believing loyalty belongs. In other words, it provides patterns that lead us to sound decisions.

As imagers of God, we must understand that God's Holy Spirit will guide our imagination to see in the spiritual realm and speak his order into our lives.

The binary choice

Go or come down? That is the choice we all must make. Jesus told his disciples - and us through those disciples - to go. Go into all the world and share the pattern of good news. *Go* means moving from one place to another. This could mean physically taking a couple of steps or using any one of any number of methods of communication to share a pattern that reveals the good news halfway around the world from where we are.

However, there's more to going than just moving. The conjunction *and* provides the purpose of going – *to disciple all nations*. It's about sharing the pattern of discipline. An evangelist will help you see the need for Christ-centered discipline in your life, while a prophet will help you stay on course – reminding of the why, when, and how.

The other option is to come down. Come down from our cross and save ourselves.

Jesus was mocked as he was dying on his cross, and taunted to come down from the cross to prove he was the Messiah. The enemy was still trying to tempt him, presumably hoping that the physical suffering he was experiencing would enhance the possibility of Jesus accepting the assertion that he didn't have to die as atonement for mankind. That he could still choose to receive all the kingdoms of the earth.

Before he died on a cross, Jesus cried out, *Eloi, Eloi, lema sabachthani! - My God, my God, why have you forsaken me?* That is the first verse of Psalm 22. While it may have sounded like he was giving in to concern for himself, every Jew who heard him would have been able to complete the Psalm, the song. They knew the remainder of the pattern:

> *[27] All the ends of the earth shall remember and turn to the Lord, and all the families of the nations shall worship before you.*
> *[28] For kingship belongs to the Lord, and he rules over the nations.*
> *[29] All the prosperous of the earth eat and worship; before him shall bow all who go down to the dust, even the one who could not keep himself alive.*
> *[30] Posterity shall serve him; it shall be told of the Lord to the coming generation;*
> *[31] they shall come and proclaim his righteousness to a people yet unborn,*
> *that he has done it. – Psalm 22:27-31 (ESV)*

Closing thoughts

During World War II, Germany bombed London daily. Yet attendance at movie theaters was at an all-time high. Some claimed people went to movies to forget the evil chaos of the bombings. I suggest they went to movies to remember – to remember a hope of peace and love.

Movies are a form of art, and as Vincent Van Gogh read to find the author of books. Three movies come to mind for me as I write.

Gone With the Wind was released in 1939. It was a highly acclaimed and awarded film, still available today on streaming services. It masterfully portrays the relationships among the characters. If filmed today, there might be more emphasis on the burning of Atlanta than on the interpersonal relationships.

The 1965 film *Doctor Zhivago* won numerous awards. It depicts the turmoil at various societal levels in Russia during the revolution that led to Communism. I've watched it multiple times and didn't fully comprehend the ending until the last viewing. A Russian military officer's relative, Yevgraf Andreyevich Zhivago, finds Tonya, believing she may be Dr. Yuri Zhivago's daughter. Yevgraf asks Tonya how she became separated from her father. She describes the chaos during the revolution, recalling how her father (Komarovsky) let go of her hand as they were running through the streets. Yevgraf assures her that Komarovsky was not her real father and that her real father (Yuri Zhivago) would *never* have let go of her hand.

Most of us today have likely seen the movie *Top Gun* (more than once). While the action captivates our attention, the best line is spoken by Commander Mike "Viper" Metcalf, played by Tom Skerritt. Maverick (Tom Cruise) arrives after the Top Gun graduation ceremony is completed. A young officer rushes into the scene to hand Viper several envelopes containing deployment orders. As Maverick receives his envelope, Viper states, *Maverick, you'll get your RIO when you get to the ship. If not, call me. I'll fly with you.* (RIO refers to Radar Intercept Officer).

We have all experienced turmoil and sought the three A's - Acceptance, Appreciation, and Approval - because of it. We've all searched for our identity. The turmoil in life is best navigated together, in unity, with resilience, giving us hope that transforms into faith, leading us to love. It's a pattern worth pursuing.

Where are you?

The two years before my father died, he shared much about his life that I was previously unaware of. I knew that his father (my grandfather) had died when my father was fourteen, but I didn't understand the struggle he faced in having to become a man at that age. After my father died, I grieved deeply. Over time, I realized that I hadn't lost him; he remained an integral part of who I am.

After Adam and Eve sinned, they heard the voice of God walking in the garden and hid.

> *[8] And they heard the sound of the LORD God walking in the garden in the cool of the day, and the man and his wife hid themselves from the presence of the*

> LORD *God among the trees of the garden.* ⁹ *But the*
> LORD *God called to the man and said to him, "Where*
> *are you?" – Genesis 3:8 (ESV)*

God called out, *Where are you?* He likely knew which bush or tree Adam was hiding behind, so the question was probably intended for Adam's reflection on his relationship with God.

The English word *sound* in Genesis 3:8 is translated from the Hebrew קוֹל (*qôl*), which primarily refers to the sound of a voice. The English word *cool* in this translation comes from the Hebrew word רוּחַ (*rûᵃḥ*) which primarily means *spirit*, or *wind*.

This theme is prevalent throughout Scripture – both the Old and New Testaments – depicting God seeking his family. There is a direct linguistic connection between Genesis 3:8 and numerous other passages in the Bible that meditate on God searching for us and us searching for God. Psalm 139 is a notable example. Isn't that what any family would do?

If you are looking for someone to journey with, contact me. I'll fly with you.

Bibliography

804 (805, W14): To Willemien van Gogh. Saint-Rémy-de-Provence, Thursday, 19 September 1889. - Vincent van Gogh Letters. (2025). Vangoghletters.org. https://vangoghletters.org/vg/letters/let804/letter.html#translation

2020 Scripture Access Statistics. (2024). Wycliffe Global Alliance. https://www.wycliffe.net/resources/statistics/

Alexander, B. K. (1987). The disease and adaptive models of addiction: A framework evaluation. Journal of Drug Issues 17, pp. 47-66.

Anderson, N. T. (2019). *The Bondage Breaker.* Harvest House Publishers.

Bullinger, E. W. (1999). *The Name of Jehovah in the Book of Esther.* Open Bible Trust ; New Berlin, Wis.

Fant, G. (2013). *The Virtues of Reading Broadly.* https://www.uu.edu/journals/renewingminds/4/RM_Issue4_Dec2013_Fant.pdf

Heiser, M. S.. (2021, October 4). *What Do The Magi and The Dead Sea Scrolls Have In Common?* YouTube. https://www.youtube.com/watch?v=52hVgs5ykFc

Heiser, M. S. (2018). *What Does God Want?* Blind Spot Press.

Hoehner, H. W. (1981). *Chronological Aspects of the Life of Christ.* Zondervan.

Holy Bible (NIV). (2011). Zondervan.

Lembke, A. (2021). *Dopamine Nation: Finding Balance in the Age of Indulgence.* Dutton.

Mast, D. L. (2015). *And David Perceived He Was King.* Xulon Press.

Michalko, M. (2007). *Thinkertoys.* The Rocks Campus Ten Speed Press.

Miller, P. E. (2014). *A Loving Life.* Crossway.

Murray, A. (2020). *Humility The Beauty of Holiness.* Outlook Verlag.

Naked Bible 016: Heiser's Laws for Bible Study. (2015, January 22). Naked Bible Podcast. https://nakedbiblepodcast.com/podcast/naked-bible-016-heisers-laws-for-bible-study-learning-to-study-the-bible-part-1/

Newton, J. D. (1989). *Uncommon Friends : life with Thomas Edison, Henry Ford, Harvey Firestone, Alexis Carrel, & Charles Lindbergh.* Harcourt Brace Jovanovich.

Oswald Chambers, & Reimann, J. (2018). *My Utmost for His Highest.* Discovery House.

Sowell, T. (2011). *Economic Facts and Fallacies.* Basic Books, Cop.

Strong, J., Brown, F., Swanson, J. A., Der, V., Robert Baker Girdlestone, & Logos Research Systems, Inc. (1998). *Old Testament Hebrew core collection.* Logos Research Systems.

The Electric Ben Franklin. (2025). Ushistory.org. https://www.ushistory.org/franklin

The Holy Bible: English Standard Version. (2016). Crossway.

The Star of Bethlehem – Exploring the evidence about the star that marked history. (n.d.). https://bethlehemstar.com/

Tozer, A. W., & Fessenden, D. E. (2003). *The Attributes of God.* Christian Publications.

Tozer, A. W., & Fessenden, D. E. (2015). *The Attributes of God. Volume 2, Deeper into the Father's heart.* Moody Publishers.

Recommended Reading

To reiterate what was stated at the beginning of this book, *Books are the windows of the world*. This author would extend a challenge to you that was extended to him by Pat Williams – read at least an hour a day. It will get you through about one book each week. This will provide you with valuable insight to share with others – an expression of love.

Spiritual Realm

The Unseen Realm by Dr. Michael S. Heiser

Reversing Hermon by Dr. Michael S. Heiser

The Silence of Adam by Dr. Larry Crabb, Don Hudson, Al Andrews

The Prophet's Manual: A Guide to Sustaining Your Prophetic Gift by John Eckhardt

Bearing God's Name: Why Sinai Still Matters by Carmen Joy Imes

Being God's Image, by Carmen Joy Imes

The Attributes of God by A.W. Tozer (two volume set)

Humility: The Beauty of Holiness by Andrew Murray

A Loving Life by Paul E. Miller

The Warrior Within by Pat Williams

How to Be like Jesus by Pat Williams

A Shepherd Looks at Psalm 23: Discovering God's Love for You by W. Phillip Keller

Victory Over The Darkness Neil T Anderson

Bondage Breaker by Neil T Anderson

Discipleship Counseling by Neil T Anderson

Until Unity by Francis Chan

Signs and Secrets of the Messiah by Rabbi Jason Sobel

The Name of Jehovah in the Book of Esther by E.W. Bullinger

And David Perceived He Was King by Dale L. Mast

The Rewards of Learning Greek & Hebrew by Catherine L. McDowell, Philip H. Towner

Prayer

The Complete Works of E.M Bounds on Prayer by E.M Bounds

With Christ in the School of Prayer by Andrew Murray

Rees Howells Intercessor: The Story of a Life Lived for God by Norman Grubb

The True Vine by Andrew Murray

A Praying Life by Paul E. Miller

Prayer Coach by James L. Nicodem

Moments with the Savior by Ken Gire

Watchman Prayer by Dutch Sheets

Praying Like Paul: Learning to Pray the Kingdom for Those You Love by Jonathan Graf

The Prayer of Jabez: Breaking Through to the Blessed Life by Bruce Wilkinson

Acts 29: Fifty Days of Prayer to Invite the Holy Spirit by Terry Teykl

Other Windows

Uncommon Friends: Life with Thomas Edison, Henry Ford, Harvey Firestone, Alexis Carrel, and Charles Lindbergh by James Newton

Thinkertoys: A Handbook of Creative-Thinking Techniques by Michael Michalko

Ideas and Information: Managing in a High-Tech World by Arno Penzias

How to be Like Rich Devos by Pat Williams

Coaching Your Kids to be Leaders by Pat Williams

Life Is Tremendous by Charlie "Tremendous" Jones

A Message to Garcia by Elbert Hubbard

Acknowledgements

Chain Breaker Ministries for demonstrating the transformation that comes from renewing our minds.

Awakening School of Theology for awakening my hunger to learn the context of original language and culture that gave us the Bible.

Vineyard Church of Central Illinois for providing encouragement to grow spiritually in a number of ways, including prophetic activation.

About the Author

Growing up in an era of western movies, Michael often dreamed of being cowboy. His parents had to wait for him to fall asleep before they could take off his boots.

A standout athlete in baseball, swimming, gymnastics, and soccer, along with a love for art, led Michael to a fifteen-year career as a professional dancer with companies in the U.S., France, and Belgium.

Michael raised and trained his own horses for a several years, and fulfilled a significant part of his dream by spending time on a 6,000 acre cattle ranch in Montana. There's something about the outside of a horse that is good for the inside of a man.

With degrees in Electronic Technology and Information Systems, Michael joined a large systems department supporting the world's largest privately owned computer network, with more than ten times the amount of data found in The Library of Congress.

Michael has served on several boards of directors for non-profit organizations. He is currently on the board of Chain Breaker Ministries in Columbus, Indiana, a Christ-centered addiction recovery residence for men. Witnessing transformation is one of the most beautiful experiences, and being part of it even more rewarding.

More recently, Michael earned a Certificate of Biblical Studies and a Certificate of Biblical History from The Awakening School of Theology, studying under Dr. Michael S. Heiser. He is currently learning Hebrew before pursuing a Certificate of Biblical Doctrine.

Michael has been blessed with numerous mentors, discovering that they arrive just as they are needed.

Speak into the darkness. Testify to the truth.

www.ingramcontent.com/pod-product-compliance
Lightning Source LLC
LaVergne TN
LVHW041322080426
835513LV00008B/548